WITHDRAWN

First–Year Teacher

A Case Study

ROBERT V. BULLOUGH, JR.

Teachers College, Columbia University
New York and London

Published by Teachers College Press, 1234 Amsterdam Avenue,
New York, NY 10027

Earlier versions of Chapters 2 and 3 appeared in the *Journal of Education for Teaching*, Vol.
13, No. 3, 1987. Material used by permission. An earlier version of Chapter 5 originally
appeared in *Teachers College Record*, Vol. 89, No. 2, Winter 1987. Reprinted with permission by *Teachers College Record*, Teachers College, Columbia University.

Library of Congress Cataloging-in-Publication Data

Bullough, Robert V., 1949–
    First-year teacher : a case study / Robert V. Bullough, Jr.
        p.   cm.
    Bibliography: p. 155
    Includes index.
    ISBN 0-8077-2935-3.   ISBN 0-8077-2934-5 (pbk.)
    1. First year teachers—United States—Case studies.   2. Seventh
grade (Education)—United States—Case studies.   I. Title.
LB2844.1.N4B85 1989
372.11′02—dc19   88-24982
                                                                                                              CIP

ISBN 0-8077-2934-5 (pbk.)
ISBN 0-8077-2935-3

Manufactured in the United States of America

94   93   92   91   90   89   1   2   3   4   5   6

TO KERRIE

Contents

Preface

I shall never forget my first year teaching ninth through twelfth graders at a large urban, public school. I spent most of the year "flying by the seat of my pants," hoping against hope that I would not only survive the year but make a difference in the lives of my students, to boot. I survived. Perhaps I even made a difference—I really do not know for certain, although from time to time I run into a former student who seems to remember me in vague but favorable terms. Since that time I have spoken with innumerable teachers and former teachers, each of whom has a story or two to tell about that first year. For most of us, the thread that unites our tales is a feeling of having done it alone, as well as a feeling of having been inadequate to meet the responsibilities thrust upon us.

Some years have passed since my first year of teaching. Eventually, I walked around to the other side of the desk and returned to school as a graduate student and, upon graduation, assumed a position as a university teacher educator, a position I have enjoyed for more than a decade. Like many other teacher educators I have worked reasonably hard to provide sensible courses for my students. I have taken seriously the aim of uniting theory and practice, and have, therefore, worked hard to carefully link planned activities in schools with the instruction offered on the university campus. I have also been committed to making certain the content in my courses has been first rate, and to this end my students have been involved in reading research relevant to their practice.

While much has gone well and I have been fortunate to have had mostly very good students, I have had a lingering concern with what happens to them once they have completed their teaching certification and assumed their first teaching job. At that point, my responsibility for them has ended, and only by chance have I found out how well or how poorly they have done during that first year.

First-Year Teacher arose out of this concern. At first I undertook the project because I wanted to better understand what was happening to my students, whether or not the work I was doing at the university was really as sensible as I thought, and whether or not there were changes in teacher education necessitated by the experience of the first-year teacher. To be sure, a book is not necessary to answer these questions (they are explored briefly in Appendix B). As I worked on the project and began sharing with colleagues, students, and teacher–friends some of the insights I was gaining, my initial purposes expanded and their priority changed. I realized that the project would be most meaningful for me if it helped beginning teachers in some small way to have a better first-year teaching experience than the one I had. But ultimately my hope is that the story told in *First-Year Teacher* will not only help make that first year a little easier, but will also help the beginning teacher discover a pathway leading to ever-increasing personal and professional competence.

Sad to say, teacher educators, many principals, and even veteran teachers (who sometimes laugh at rookie innocence and naiveté) pay little attention to first-year teachers. The feeling of going it alone, which I had as a first-year teacher, continues to be a common experience. The importance of that year not only to the beginning teacher but to the profession as well is somehow often missed. For good or ill, the struggle through the first year creates a pattern of behavior and understanding that is played out in subsequent years — habits develop, ideas begin to harden, content settles. How well or how poorly the beginning teacher gets through the year has a profound importance for future personal and professional development. The first year of teaching sets a foundation upon which is built either a professional educator, or something else that masquerades in teachers' clothing and cashes a teacher's checks.

Throughout the length of this project numerous individuals have been helpful. I would like to thank my father and colleague, Professor Robert V. Bullough Sr., who has read and commented on most of the manuscript and supported me unconditionally these many years. Professor Donald Kauchak, also a colleague, has been an extremely thoughtful and helpful critic. I benefited immensely from his insightful questions and comments. I also benefited from the critical comments of Professor Renee Clift, who kindly read and commented on the entire manuscript. Also, thanks are in order to Professors Earl Harmer and Ladd Holt, and to Ms. Ruth Symmes, herself a first-year teacher, for their thoughtful comments on portions of the manuscript. My wife, Dawn Ann, deserves tribute as well for her interest in and support for the study. In addition, I owe a debt of gratitude to Professor Ralph

Reynolds, Chair of the Department of Educational Studies, who willingly provided essential resources in support of the study.

Finally, my most profound debt is to Kerrie, who, by any measure, is a remarkable and courageous person. I continue to marvel that she was willing to allow me to spend so much time in her classroom, through both good and bad times, and that she so openly shared her thoughts and feelings. This book is dedicated to her.

Introduction

First-Year Teacher presents a case study of the first year (and the first semester of the second year) of teaching by a seventh-grade public school teacher. The teacher selected for study, Kerrie, obviously was not "every teacher," but in a great many ways her experience of the first year of teaching was typical. Certainly the problems she faced were, for the most part, common ones. The setting too, while somewhat unusual, was more typical than not. But along with commonality comes uniqueness; obviously any two teachers or any two schools will be different in important ways. Just as Kerrie encountered the common problems of beginning teachers, she also faced problems that were unique to her and to the teaching context. Because of this, a word needs to be said, before describing Kerrie and the setting in detail, about the value of case studies in teacher education to students in this field. The utility of *First-Year Teacher* should thereby become apparent.

Lee Shulman (1986) lists five types of knowledge about teaching: empirical propositions; moral propositions; conceptual inventions, clarifications, and critiques; technologies or procedural protocols; and exemplars of practice or malpractice. The latter are "normally case descriptions of teachers, classrooms, or schools. They do not claim empirical generalizability. They are presented as instances or exemplars, documenting how education was accomplished (or stymied) by a particular group of teachers and students in a particular place" (p. 27).

Interest in cases and case studies of teaching has been increasing recently. It is being realized that they have a unique role to play in the study of education (Shulman & Colbert, 1987). Clearly they are an effective means for communicating ideas about practice, but they are much more. Cases and case studies are stories that, in their telling, invite the reader to question and explore personal values and understandings:

- What if I were in a similar situation?
- What would I do and why would I do it?

- How are my values and understandings the same as, or different from, those presented in the case study?
- Are my understandings any better?
- Are my values likely to get me into some kind of difficulty?

Written cases and case studies are a means by which educators can explore how others have confronted problems similar to their own. They are also a means by which to identify potential problems and a vehicle by which to begin thinking them through. In these ways they can influence the basis on which teaching decisions are or will be made. Again quoting Shulman (1986):

> Fenstermacher argues that educating a teacher is not a matter of inculcating a knowledge base in the form of a specific set of teaching skills and competencies. Rather, to educate a teacher is to influence the premises on which a teacher bases practical reasoning about teaching in specific situations. (p. 32)

Cases and case studies have this potential. They have it in part because of their unique pedagogical power:

> Most individuals find specific cases more powerful influences on their decisions than impersonally presented empirical findings, even though the later constitute 'better' evidence. Although principles are powerful, cases are memorable, and lodge in memory as the basis for later judgments. (p. 32)

My hope is that *First-Year Teacher* will have such an influence.

Eight chapters follow, along with a brief conclusion and three appendixes. In addition, each chapter ends with a list of questions and a few activities, for both teacher education students and beginning teachers. Chapter 1 introduces Kerrie and the school within which she worked and presents the developmental themes that will run throughout the book. Chapters 2 and 3 focus on Kerrie's and other beginning teachers' most serious problem: planning for and dealing with discipline and management. Chapter 4 describes Kerrie's struggle with the five most common problems faced by beginning teachers — including, in addition to discipline, dealing with individual differences, motivation, assessing students' work, and parental relations — and the skills she developed to deal with them. Chapter 5 presents the coping strategies she used, and concludes with a discussion of teacher burnout. Chapter 6 explores Kerrie's changing understanding of teacher professionalism in the light of her future development as a teacher. Chapter 7 describes Kerrie's teaching early in the second year, as a basis for making comparisons with the first year. Chapter 8 addresses problems Kerrie faced that arose from accountability pressures, and teacher mentoring and evaluation. For readers interested in methodological questions, Appendix A briefly explores some of the issues raised by this study. Appendix B focuses on teacher education and its influence on professional development, raising questions that deserve the careful attention of both teacher educators and teacher education students. Appendix C provides the beginning teacher with some advice on selecting a school to work in and some suggestions for facilitating the first year of teaching.

1 Setting the Stage

Kerrie, as a first-year teacher, was selected for the study from among a cohort group of 22 university students pursuing secondary school certification for whom I had the primary instructional responsibility for a year. I worked with her in curriculum and instruction courses, a seminar designed to deal with the problems of student teaching, as well as student teaching itself. I selected her for three primary reasons. First, she was among the better students in the teacher education cohort group. Specifically, she possessed several of the qualities and abilities frequently identified with public school teaching success: enthusiasm, a sense of humor, intelligence, and the ability to communicate clearly and to vary instructional methods. In short, she was likely to do well. Based on years of reading education literature, my impression is that too little attention has been given to those teachers who do well in our schools, and that from them we can learn something quite different from what we can learn from the study of failure. Second, Kerrie was employed early enough to have had sufficient time to prepare for the school year without being rushed. Third, and perhaps most important, she was willing to commit the time and energy necessary for the study to take place.

Before the beginning of the school year, I interviewed Kerrie to gain information about how she saw her role as teacher and about any concerns she might have had about beginning to teach. Following the initial interview, each week I observed her teaching at a different time of day. At the conclusion of a school day during which an observation had taken place, I conducted an interview with her. Through questioning I attempted to get at the thinking behind various observed teacher actions. In addition, I asked questions that arose from my analysis of the interview transcripts, which were coded to identify emerging themes. Once again, my attempt was to understand why certain actions were undertaken or decisions made. In addition, at mid-year, I interviewed the principal and four randomly selected students, two boys and two girls, from Kerrie's classes. The student interviews were conducted to check my perceptions of how Kerrie was being received by the students and to gain additional insight into the meaning of classroom events.

Finally, observations and interviews were continued into Kerrie's second year of teaching to determine if and in what manner the patterns of the first year persisted or changed.

Throughout this book I quote at length from my interviews with Kerrie and also provide comments from the principal and student interviews. My questions during the interviews are shown in italics. Except for Kerrie's, all names used are fictitious.

Personal characteristics — attitudes, beliefs, dispositions — are important factors influencing how an individual teacher responds to a given teaching context (Goodman, 1985; Zeichner, 1986). They form interpretative lenses, cognitive schema, through which the teacher makes sense of the teaching environment. As such, they help establish what is understood as right, reasonable, and proper. In order to understand how and why Kerrie responded to her teaching environment, it is first necessary to know something about Kerrie.

KERRIE

Kerrie was a 29-year-old mother of two. She began college after her own children were in school and she began to feel the need to start a career outside of the home. She chose teaching for a variety of typical reasons. Her mother's decision to begin a teaching career following the raising of her family served as a model for Kerrie's decision. And, as a public school student in the Midwest and West she had several teachers who inspired her to think of teaching as a career: "I had this Mr. King. This is where I fell in love with history!" Through people like Mr. King, she developed a profound respect for teachers and an interest in the teacher role as she understood it: "They were rulers in their kingdoms, I guess. [It] sounds kind of funny. They had a territory; it was their's. They could rule it however they wanted within limits. They were the bosses." These were important influences, but apparently they only confirmed a decision made very early in Kerrie's life. Indeed, Kerrie could not remember a time in her life when she had not wanted to be a teacher:

I always wanted to be a teacher. [As a child, my girlfriend and I] played school all summer long. [I was always the] teacher. We had a nonexistent [class] that we were handing out work to. Sometimes we'd drag in my girlfriend's brothers to be the students. They'd have to be sent to the principal all the time because they were bad. I liked organizing things like my desk. Getting my mom to buy me a roll book. Going around looking through my house at things that I could put on my TV tray which would be my desk. Lining up chairs. Assigning names . . . writing on the chalkboard.

Each of these factors was important to Kerrie's decision to become a teacher; they also shaped her understanding of the teacher role. Teachers were knowledgeable and fun people, were in charge of large numbers of students who frequently needed disciplining, and spent a good deal of their time organizing materials and activities. But, as she matured, perhaps the most important factor in shaping how Kerrie understood teaching, particularly during the beginning months of her first year in the field, was her experience as a mother and the high value she placed on nurturing. This influence was prominently expressed in various ways. It was present in how she approached planning throughout much of the year: "I think I bounce most of my ideas off my children." It was present in her statements about goals, where the most important outcomes centered on student growth and development and on establishing warm and caring relations: "It makes you feel good to see that they're happy." Further, as the year progressed she was especially pleased with her morning students because they became "like a big family" and a "cohesive group." And it was present in her language and in her descriptions of what she found most satisfying about teaching. She was thrilled, for instance, with the outcome of a student evaluation she administered: "I had an awful lot [of students] say 'you're my favorite teacher,' or 'you're the best teacher I ever had.' That's heartwarming." And, "Of course, 'like' isn't everything but it sure does feel good to have your kids like you."

Success as a student, a mother, and a student teacher, as well as in various church-related teaching responsibilities, gave Kerrie confidence, as she approached her first year of teaching, that she would be a good teacher. According to the principal, her confidence was one of the reasons she was selected for the job over the other applicants. Drawing on notes taken at the time of his interview with her, he commented that "she presented herself very well . . . she was confident as I talked to her." As the year progressed this initial impression was strengthened. "She's got confidence," he said, "at least as I watch her and as the kids watch her there is no doubt that she knows what she's doing. She is confident in front of the class, handles herself very well, and works hard." Confidence was important to Kerrie because even in the very difficult times she encountered throughout the year she remained firm in the conviction that she could and would succeed.

Four additional qualities bear heavily on how Kerrie responded to the teaching context. First, she was extremely well organized and took pleasure in planning. Second, she was not a worrier. When a problem confronted her about which she could do little, if anything, she generally was able to set it aside or mull it around without becoming consumed by it. Third, she was not a complainer. It bothered her, for example, to listen to other teachers gripe about their work. "I'm not a bitcher, I don't think. It just disturbs me that [teachers are] always . . . tearing down our profession by the complaining we do." And later, it's "really hard [to take]. It's like getting mothers together. They talk about all the labor pains they've had and the children. This birth and that birth. It's the same with teachers when they get together. That's kind of hard [to listen to]." Finally, Kerrie was, as she put it, "a loner."

> I'm really a loner. I mean, it's funny because sometimes it will be fifth period before I even say anything to [the teacher who shares my classroom area]. I'm not someone who goes around and visits with everyone. I'd rather sit down and read a book! It's my personal makeup. I like to be left alone.

CHARACTERISTICS OF SCHOOLS

Schools differ, but schooling, as John Goodlad notes, is everywhere very much the same (Bullough, 1987; Goodlad, 1984). It is this sameness that sets schools apart from other types of institutions, like shopping centers and fire stations. The sameness of schools brings with it a set of problems with which all teachers must grapple and in some fashion resolve. Schools are organized hierarchically, with principals at the top, then teachers, and students at the bottom. Large numbers of students are sifted, sorted according to age and ability, and apportioned among teachers. In this process in secondary schools, students are typically tracked into high-, medium-, and low-ability groupings, particularly in the sciences, mathematics, English, and foreign languages. Indeed, the experience of tracking is virtually universal (Oakes, 1985). Subject matter is packaged, presented, and tested. Students are constantly evaluated, with the result that individual competitiveness is highly rewarded. The day is neatly divided into periods the beginning and ending of which are signaled by bells or buzzers. Interruptions—whether announcements over the intercom or students breaking into class presentations with notes from the office—are commonplace and impossible to prevent.

While these characteristics are common to schooling, individual schools do differ, and these differences are of genuine importance to teachers, particularly first-year teachers. The first-year teacher, upon first walking through the school's doors, enters more than a building. As a complex, active bearer of habits, values, and beliefs—as a unique person—he or she enters a set of established roles, relationships, ways of behaving, and understandings (including a language used to talk about the school, students, teachers, and the like) that give a particular school its unique character. For the most part these are taken for granted, and principals, parents, students, and other teachers urge conformity. In this setting the novice teacher must negotiate a place that is personally and professionally satisfying, as well as institutionally acceptable, which is difficult even in the best of circumstances. Small differences among schools may make substantial differences in the kind and quality of professional life that is forged by the novice teacher. It makes a great deal of difference, for example, if the administration is supportive of teachers and has high expectations for student performance. It makes a great deal of difference if the students come to school expecting to learn. And, it makes a great deal of difference if classrooms are clean, materials available, and other faculty members willing to share.

ROCKY MOUNTAIN JUNIOR HIGH SCHOOL

The specific school context into which Kerrie entered was Rocky Mountain Junior High School. It was built in 1980 in the middle of what was once a thriving agricultural area that urban sprawl eventually engulfed. Pressed between modest but mostly newer homes was a large, run-down trailer park; a few small, cluttered farms; a sprinkling of small businesses, including convenience stores, gas stations, and fast food restaurants; an occasional remnant of what was once light industry; and fields torn up in various stages of development. The student population of 970 was composed of working-class, and lower- and middle-class students. Additionally, a few "cowboys," distinguished by their dress and manners, remained. About 10 percent of Kerrie's students fell into one or another ethnic minority category. It was a good school (according to Kerrie), where the students were, for the most part, well behaved.

Kerrie taught seventh-grade core as part of a three-person team, which is an atypical arrangement. She had two relatively stable groups of students for three periods each: English, social studies, and reading. The 23 students in the morning class—two thirds of whom were boys—were identified as remedial according to the standardized achievement tests used for grouping. This group's reading scores ranged from third to about grade level. The afternoon class, bulging with 36 students, was deemed "average," on and slightly above grade level. The team leader taught the "advanced" core, while the third team member taught an additional "average" section. As in other American secondary schools, the day was neatly divided into periods, in this case, 7 periods of 43 minutes each, followed by an enrichment period during which teachers were available to give special help to students needing or desiring it. Buzzers marked the beginning and ending of a period, with a five-minute break between periods. Twenty-five minutes were set aside for a lunch break.

Classroom

Kerrie's classroom was quite unusual, and a source of some persistent problems. She was assigned to one of three large rooms called a "pod," formed by subdividing a huge open area. The rooms were separated by carpeted floor-to-ceiling movable walls and were joined in one corner by a small open area just large enough to allow noise to transfer easily from one room to the others. Access to the other two rooms was gained by crossing Kerrie's classroom and this open area.

The ease with which sound traveled among the rooms made the three teachers hypersensitive to noise as a factor in selecting or creating learning activities. As Kerrie commented, "You cannot imagine. One kid makes a noise in the other class and it sets them all off." And, "I'm going to be stricter about general behavior in the classroom. It makes me mad when the other classes are noisy, so, turnabout." The pressure was to avoid noisy activities.

The classroom arrangement allowed other pressures to develop as well. The close physical proximity of the classrooms and the existence of the open area linking them enabled the teachers easily to observe one another teaching, with the result that, willingly or unwillingly, Kerrie was under constant, albeit generally friendly, surveillance. Initially, being watched was a source of some insecurity. Kerrie felt she needed to please the team leader and, to a degree, she felt she was in some ways in competition with her. Kerrie's temptation was to compare her own performance with that of the veteran team leader when both were doing similar activities. Often the comparison proved unfavorable, with the result that Kerrie was relieved when they were not doing the same kinds of activities: "I like to do things by myself. There's no competition, kind of, to put yourself up against, especially [when I'm doing activities for the] first time." The physical arrangement of the three rooms also presented problems to students, who easily could observe the other classes and would often give in to the temptation to stop what they were supposed to be doing in order to gaze through the open area.

Teaching Assignment

Kerrie was the new kid on the block and, as such, of the three team members, she received the most difficult teaching assignment, while the most senior teacher, the team leader, received the "best" assignment. As a beginning teacher, what could she do? Obtaining preferred teaching assignments was serious business within the school, and the teachers quietly fought over them. During Kerrie's second year, and following the transfer of one of the team members, to her delight she was assigned two "average" reading groups while the new team member was assigned the low-ability group. The connection between preferred teaching assignments and teacher hierarchy was one of the reasons there continued to be a commitment to ability grouping, even as evidence mounts that educationally it is a questionable practice (see Grant & Rothenberg, 1986; Oakes, 1985).[1] The principal observed that if the teachers wished, they could have altered the arrangement. "I have," he remarked, "teachers that say 'no [to homogeneous grouping], I don't want it that way.' My philosophy is that if you can show me that what you want to do is better, then you can do what you say you want to do. I have some teachers that don't ability group." But Kerrie's team leader did not want a change. She preferred teaching the advanced core.

Students

The wise visitor to Rocky Mountain Junior High comes while class is in session and all is orderly and well contained. Only the foolish or inordinately brave dare venture the hallways between classes, when they are alive with the vitality of youth that so frightens, yet entices, us adults. When the buzzer sounds, signaling the conclusion of a class period, the only secure spots for adults who wish to avoid being swept away are in corners or near the teachers responsible for hall patrol. The hallways are narrow and dark, and the traffic flows at a furious, swirling pace. It is orderly chaos. Everywhere there is laughter, pushing, shoving, and occasional hitting and hugging as boys and girls test out sex roles. The insides of locker doors are unashamedly decorated with large fan magazine pictures of the latest "hunk." Both sexes are adorned with the trappings of adulthood, without the physique to bear them either as gracefully or, occasionally, as alluringly as intended. Style matters. Tight jeans (which are oddly loose) are complemented by wobbly high-heels that enclose huge feet. Boat-size sneakers are carefully color-coordinated with bulky sweaters. Creatively applied make-up masks skin on

---

[1] A brief review of the research is presented in "Organizing Classes of Ability" (1987).

the verge of erupting. The noise and chaos continue, and then, suddenly, end with a buzzer just as quickly as they began. Silence engulfs the hallways, and the visitor is left alone, except for the maintenance worker who quietly pushes a broom up the hallway, removing a few discarded reminders of what just transpired. What lingers is a feeling that these young people are very powerful and that it is something of a miracle that the school is able to direct their energy at all, let alone in productive ways.

Indeed, students are a powerful influence in shaping the teaching context. Their mere presence is a constant reminder to teachers that disorder is always lurking just around the corner so they must be constantly on alert; in all schools discipline and management are central concerns. But the power of students is not always so obvious; at times it is subtle, often unnoticed. Of particular importance to beginning teachers is their influence as socializing agents. As Doyle (1983) and other researchers have noted, through playing out an internalized student role, a role taken for granted, young people press teachers to conform to their own expectations of what is appropriate teacher behavior. Teachers who demand too much or even too little will find themselves in a struggle over who will establish and control the classroom learning climate.[2]

Through not turning in assignments or not completing assigned work, Kerrie's low-ability students pressed her to lower her expectations. Such pressures are encouraged by homogeneous grouping of lower-ability students, with the result that lower student self-esteem and performance become institutionalized (Oakes, 1985). Homogeneous ability grouping often also has unfortunate effects on average-ability students, who wonder why they are deemed "average." What is "wrong" with them? Kerrie also faced this problem:

> My afternoon class will often say—the morning class just by looking around know that they're not the brilliant people—the afternoon class, though, will ask, all the time, "Are we gifted?" I'll say "No," because they know [the team leader's class] is. Then they'll ask "Are we advanced core?" I'll say, "No." They should know that, I'm sure they know that. But every now and again they'll come up and say "Are we the advanced core?" "No. We just do the same things as they do, pretty much."

The difficulty Kerrie faced was to get these students to perform at a high level when, by virtue of their placement and low expectations, many of

---

[2]That students pressure teachers to lower expectations is widely recognized. They may also pressure them to raise their expectations. An instance of this kind of pressure is reported in Connell, Ashenden, Kessler, and Dowsett (1982).

them believed that they were incapable of such performance. A quote from one of the student interviews illustrates the difficulty well:

> [Kerrie] just gives the same amount of work, mostly, [as other teachers], except for [the team leader's] class. They assign from chapter to chapter every day in English because they are advanced. *What does that mean?* They're in advanced core. *It doesn't mean they are any smarter, does it?* Well, it means they got better grades in fifth grade so they got to take the test. And if they got good on that test they could go into advanced [core]. *How does that make you feel?* Fine, I didn't want to go into advanced [core]. *How come?* Gives you too much work.

The expectation of this student was that he should not have to work; he did a minimal amount and was satisfied with it. For him, attending school — except during lunch and between classes — was akin to having a mild cold, something to be endured in anticipation of a time when it will have run its course and health returns.

In addition, Kerrie's students were quite unsophisticated compared with those students in the advanced core. Many of them had not fully mastered the student game, as Kerrie explains:

> She (the team leader) gives instruction [to the advanced core students] and they all listen. Then they break into groups and they know just what to do. Mine, only half of them listen and I have to give more instructions. So, they are less independent that way. They rely less on each other. Or else they're so dumb they ask the wrong people [for help]. Instead of asking those whom they should ask, they ask those they shouldn't and then they get the wrong answers! For example, someone today came up and asked me something like, "If we get a 'B' we don't have to take the test, right?" I said, "Who said that? Well, do you trust him? What do you think?"

Their lack of sophistication also manifested itself in the inability of many students to "read" the classroom. "They don't take signals," Kerrie complained, "that's basically [the problem]. How long should I stand up [in front of the class] waiting for them to shut up?" As Doyle noted (1986), more able students typically engage in off-task behavior at times when it is unlikely to be visible or disruptive, such as during transitions or at the end of a lesson segment. Less able students, in contrast, act out in the middle of lessons; they simply do not know when to engage in off-task behavior with impunity. And so, less sophisticated students get into trouble with teachers for doing what other students do, but for doing it at the wrong time or place. Privileges are lost as a result.

I let them come in [and sit where they want until] I can't stand them talking anymore. I try out this freedom thing that I think is going to work but then I have to give them a seating chart. If they're noisy, then I'll move them. Then, just like that, they have a referral [to the vice principal's office].

Fortunately, this lack of sophistication, particularly in the students in the morning classes, was not entirely a bad quality. Most of the time Kerrie found their unpredictability and their naiveté endearing.

This is going to sound kind of screwy but my morning classes—all I can think of is they're kind of awkward and tentative but they make great leaps. Shocking leaps sometimes. They will catch onto things that I have to drag out of [my afternoon class at times]. And, they are much more cuddly.

Finally, the sheer numbers of students Kerrie had to deal with should be noted. Clearly, class size makes a difference to teachers in the kinds of activities that they plan and the kinds of relationships they are able to develop with young people. Large class size also increased Kerrie's control and management problems, as will be discussed later at length. These are frequently mentioned by beginning teachers as their most serious problems (Veenman, 1984).

Work Relations

The faculty member directly responsible for helping Kerrie during her first year was the team leader who was to serve as her mentor, but without formal mentoring responsibilities. Selection as a team leader was made by the principal based on seniority, willingness to do the job, and ability. Since there was no remuneration for the position, willingness to do the job was an especially important selection criterion.

The team leader took a hands-off policy toward Kerrie throughout most of the year. She would answer questions, offer materials, but seldom volunteered assistance. The only occasions early in the year when she volunteered information were those few times when Kerrie appeared on the verge of breaking a school rule as, for instance, when she naively planned a student party. Virtually no one within the school explained to Kerrie either school rules or how the school functioned. She was, for the most part, left on her own (as are most first-year teachers).

Kerrie was given a clue as to what her relationship with the team leader would be, prior to the beginning of the school year. Only begrudgingly did the team leader agree to meet with Kerrie to discuss Kerrie's teaching assignment:

[The team leader] knew I was coming last spring. I had to call her in the summer to come and meet me over [at the school]. She acted like, "This is my summer vacation, but OK." That was hard! I mean, here I am going into a new situation, odd person out, and taking someone's place [and she doesn't want to meet with me].

As the year progressed, despite their having adjoining rooms and being almost constantly within sight of one another, Kerrie received virtually no feedback on her performance. She found this troubling: "It's her job—except she is not getting paid for it! If there were a new teacher in with me, even next year, or any year, I would certainly have more to say about how things were going." Apparently, the team leader's behavior was unexceptional within the school; as the principal explained: "[The team leaders in the school] are the way they are largely because of what I feel they ought to do. They don't get any extra money for [being team leaders]. I don't expect a super amount, I really don't."

Of necessity, the team met periodically to plan upcoming units and to share materials. This was not, however, a time for discussing problems or for giving feedback. Rather, the task was to fill out a calendar of events and decide who would use what materials when. On the face of it, a team meeting would have appeared to be an opportune moment to be supportive or to give some well-intentioned but critical feedback. It was not. Indeed, while reflecting on the first seven months of school, Kerrie could identify only two instances when she had been given positive feedback from her colleagues on her teaching performance, and not a single instance of negative or critical feedback.

A couple of times [I've been stroked]. We're kind of a hallway through here and into the outside. People have come in and just seen things in the room or asked about the newspaper—because kids were carrying around newspapers [done in class] for a long time—I had some comments on that that were positive. *In the whole year, that's it?* Yes, I would say so, at least that I would chalk up as strokes.

Clearly, Kerrie was on her own during much of the school year even though, ostensibly, she was part of a team of teachers. The expectation appeared to be that first-year teachers either sink or swim (see Darling-Hammond, 1985).

Much has been written about teacher isolation and its effects on teachers. Teaching is, as Lortie (1975) and others have noted, a lonely profession. It is even difficult to visit a teacher at the "other end of the corridor" (Freedman et al., 1983). What is somewhat remarkable about Kerrie's situation was that physically, at least, she was not isolated.

After all, the team leader had an unobstructed view into Kerrie's room. And, in fact, Kerrie learned much from the opportunity to observe the team leader across the open space joining their rooms. Nevertheless, their interactions were minimal. One partial explanation of this phenomenon is that teachers do not expect to interact. The role of the teacher is built around the norm of an individual teacher working with an individual class separated from other teachers and other classes, a view entirely consistent with Kerrie's tendency to be a loner. Teacher autonomy, therefore, is closely associated with teacher isolation (Bullough, 1987; Bullough & Gitlin, 1986). Being alone in a classroom brings with it a feeling of being autonomous, in control. Rather than team teach, for example, team members divide up the curriculum so that each may function independently of the others. This helps explain how it was possible that Kerrie found out only by accident that her classes were several lessons behind the others in English at mid-year and that she needed to speed up. Clearly, teacher attitudes, beliefs, and values help shape the teaching context.

Principal

Principals establish and maintain the academic tone of their schools and are extremely important to faculty morale (Goodlad, 1984). Kerrie's principal trusted teachers and expected them to behave and perform professionally. Nevertheless, he wanted a quiet, orderly school and to this end monitored his teachers very closely. For example, during the second week of the school year Kerrie misread the schedule of when she was supposed to do her hall duty. She went to the assigned location but at the wrong time. The next day she found in her box a note saying she missed her appointed assignment. Kerrie thought the principal's note appropriate and later explained to him what had happened. Yet, as she spoke of the incident, she betrayed an ambivalence toward the principal's actions. It was, she thought, his job to watch over teachers, as teachers watched over students: "He keeps tabs on us very well," she asserted. "I think it is his job. It's like me walking up and down the aisles." But she did not like it; it was a necessary evil: "Now, this isn't saying it doesn't bother me, but it tends to keep you on your toes, I think." While she did not believe she needed watching, she suspected that other teachers did, although she was uncertain about this. Later in the year, in fact, she discovered that the principal was working closely with two teachers in particular: He spent considerable time with a first-year teacher who improved dramatically after having had serious problems with classroom control. And he spent an inordinate amount of time documenting the inadequate performance of a veteran teacher whom he hoped to terminate. To Kerrie, these two instances confirmed the importance of the principal's keeping tabs on the faculty.

Because she performed adequately during her first year of teaching, Kerrie received very little attention from the principal, even though she was formally evaluated twice during the year as required by district policy. Because she did well, the principal could spend his time on relatively more pressing matters, of which there were many. Prior to the first evaluation Kerrie was worried, but her concern gave way to disappointment following their meeting.

> I was really nervous about it, but it turned out not to be anything. He handed me a blank [evaluation form] and said, "This is what the evaluation form looks like." I thought, "Oh, this is the precursor [to the evaluation]." Then, a few minutes later, after he'd discussed it, he said, "Here's your evaluation." Hands me one that's filled out. Then he said he's glad I'm teaching here and he really likes me. Thinks I'm doing a good job. That was about it. No problems.

On reflection, she was bothered that she would be evaluated based on so little personal contact. "He has cruised through the classroom quite a few times . . . like every couple of weeks he walks in. At the first of the year he did come in and stay for about five minutes." She had hoped for more helpful feedback, feedback that said something more than: "Orderly class, is well organized, well prepared." While she appreciated being told that she was doing a good job, she learned nothing from the evaluation that would help her become a better teacher, and this was disappointing. "I felt good about [the comment] because I knew it was true, but I already knew that!"

District Curriculum and Testing

Kerrie's school district had established an outcomes-based program composed of lists of behavioral goal statements and tests tied to those goals for English and reading (see Bullough, Goldstein, & Holt, 1984). In the social studies area the state had established a core curriculum, which, in reality, was little more than a list of topics to be taught. The expectation was that Kerrie would teach the district's programs, but, ironically, no one followed up on the initial introduction to the programs before the school year began. "All I can say about it is that we are supposed to be teaching [these programs] (laughter). I really don't know anything about [them]. They're (the school and district administrators) really not hitting on them." Throughout Kerrie's entire first year of teaching, virtually no one within the school encouraged her to follow the district guidelines — nor monitored her program — but, inadvertently, she did by using the materials presented to her by the team leader. (The situation changed dramatically during her second year, however, as discussed in Chapter 8.)

The principal's expectation was clear: "What I have said to my teachers is that these goals are the things that our kids are tested on. That's the thing I expect you to teach. I expect your curriculum to include those major goals." This expectation had been in full force when the team leader first developed the curriculum that was presented to Kerrie to teach. Gradually, Kerrie recognized the fit between what had been given to her to teach — particularly the textbooks selected — and the district and state guidelines and standardized achievement tests. Her task was to cover the suggested topics — she did not worry about meeting specific objectives — and the test scores would take care of themselves.

Pace of Work

In the best of circumstances, teaching is hectic, but for first-year teachers it sometimes borders on the frantic. "It just drives me crazy," Kerrie remarked, "there's so much to do!" The responsibilities of teachers seem endless: managing large numbers of students, finding materials, making up handouts, grading, "logging" student behavior for counselors, meeting with parents, responding to student requests for help, and so on. For the most part these tasks are the same for novice teachers as for experienced, expert teachers. The difference is, of course, that experienced teachers presumably have learned how to do all these things expeditiously. For beginning teachers, even simple tasks often prove enervating as they struggle to learn to use their time effectively and how to discriminate between important and comparatively less important demands, let alone try to cover all the required material. This was certainly true for Kerrie, with the result that, except for comparatively brief moments, she sprinted throughout the year.

Summary

This was the work setting that Kerrie entered for her first year of teaching: Her classroom was linked to two other rooms by an open area that brought with it some unique problems. Noise easily transferred from one area into the next. Other teachers could easily observe Kerrie teaching. And students were frequently distracted by the activities of other classes. Half of her classes were designated low ability; the other half were labeled "average." In both groups a large number of students expected to do very little school work. On the whole the faculty was friendly but not particularly supportive of beginning teachers. The team leader, who had responsibility for working with and helping Kerrie, shared materials and occasionally instructional ideas when asked, but was not inclined to give feedback on Kerrie's performance or to volunteer suggestions. Indeed, throughout much of the year she maintained a respectful distance that shrunk somewhat only near year's end. The principal, despite being extraordinarily busy, kept a careful watch to make certain all teachers performed their assigned duties. Kerrie was no exception. Upon entering the school Kerrie was presented with a curriculum that she was supposed to teach. In social studies it was an outline of topics; in English it was a text; and in reading it included a list of novels. Additionally, in all three areas the team leader gave her copies of units that had been taught the year before. Despite all these materials, how she taught them — and even what she taught — was ultimately her decision. She was, however, reminded that near the end of the year all students would be tested. Finally, teachers in Rocky Mountain Junior High School worked hard. They maintained a rapid pace, which was necessary if they hoped to cover the required material, let alone fulfill the wide range of responsibilities that came with the job.

STAGES OF TEACHER DEVELOPMENT

There is a common perception that a person is fully qualified to teach upon receiving certification. The implicit message is extremely unfortunate and encourages abandonment of beginning teachers. It simply is not the case that upon certification anyone is fully able to do all that is necessary to develop and implement a successful plan of instruction for several dozen students. The skills and understandings essential to such a task take years to perfect, and some "teachers" never perfect them. Every teacher needs help, lots of it. Fortunately, researchers are beginning to acknowledge what practitioners have long known: There are dramatic differences between novice teachers and experienced, expert teachers. For example, experts are more sensitive to the teaching context, they are more opportunistic as planners, they recognize patterns in student behavior, and they appear to know their classes even before they meet them (Berliner, 1986). But how does one become expert? What is the process a beginning teacher goes through in the move toward teaching competence? Of this, comparatively little is known.

Like learning any complex art or craft, becoming a teacher is a developmental process characterized by devastating disappointments and failures, as well as sparkling moments of success. In thinking about Kerrie's first year developmentally, I have found the stages proposed by Kevin Ryan (1986) to be helpful. Discussion of these stages will run throughout *First-Year Teacher*. Drawing on and extending the work of Francis Fuller, Ryan argues that on the way to professional competence teachers go through four loose but identifiable stages: A "fantasy" stage, a "survival" stage, a "mastery" stage, and finally an "impact" stage. The fantasy stage begins when an individual "starts to think seriously about becoming a teacher" (p. 10). During the fantasy stage the imagination runs wild with images of spellbound young people eagerly awaiting the next teacher pronouncement. The neophyte imagines himself or herself being just like or better than the best teachers he or she has had and certainly very different from the worst teachers. But there is a dark side to the fantasy stage: fleeting images of a class defiantly refusing to do as told; images of spit wads thudding and sticking against the blackboard, unpleasant reminders of student hostility and disrespect. The fantasy stage is interrupted by student teaching but, for those who continue in the resolve to teach, it is but a brief hiatus. Fantasizing is very much a part of the anticipation of the first "real" teaching job, as we shall see in the chapter that follows; indeed, it significantly shapes the transition from university student to the teacher role, sometimes leading to what one researcher calls "transition shock" (Corcoran, 1981).

Upon beginning their first job, beginning teachers quickly discover that "real" teaching and student teaching are remarkably different experiences. Thus the shock. To note a few common differences: Typically they student taught in classrooms where instructional and management routines were already established. They enjoyed the support and attention of a cooperating teacher who was genuinely interested in their success, if for no other reason than to make certain they did not foul up the students' or teacher's programs too severely. And they had cooperating teachers' units to draw upon, even if they did not like them. First-year teachers can count on none of this. Quickly they discover that in various ways their experience has been inadequate, or perhaps just irrelevant, to the tasks facing them. The fantasy crumbles.

The discovery of inadequacy ushers in the survival stage of teaching, the fight for one's professional life. This fight is the central focus of

Chapter 3, which deals with the serious discipline and management problems — the most common problems faced by beginning teachers — that Kerrie began having shortly after the start of the school year. Most frequently the survival stage sets in between October and the Christmas break, though it might come at virtually any point. The "typical pattern is for teachers to be lulled into complacency by what they perceive as early successes and then to work themselves into difficulties during one of the early months of the school year" (Ryan, 1986, p. 14). This stage may last only a short while or continue until the end of the year. It may be intense or relatively mild. And it may be set off by a dramatic series of events or by what appears to be a seemingly innocuous problem with one student. In any case, come it must, as it did for Kerrie, and through it the beginning teacher either succeeds in establishing a renewed sense of identity and self-worth, or is crushed and becomes disenchanted with teaching and angry with students.

For most teachers the survival stage is over by February; for many, like Kerrie, it ends sooner. The mastery stage, as described by Ryan, is the "craft stage, where the new teacher begins to learn the craft of teaching in a step-by-step fashion" (p. 14). At this point, having generally gained control over discipline and management concerns and developed a measure of security in the classroom, the beginning teacher focuses, more or less systematically, on the improvement of particular teaching skills and of content. At this stage achieving improved student learning replaces achieving good student behavior as the dominating focus (Fuller & Brown, 1975). The discussion of Kerrie's movement into the mastery stage of teaching begins in the latter part of Chapter 3 and is covered more fully in subsequent chapters. Finally, a word should be said about the impact stage of teaching. This stage is not within the grasp of a beginning teacher. It is here where we would expect to find experienced, expert teachers, who have mastered the skills of teaching, are actively engaged professionally, and are capable of articulating the grounds of their expertise.

Kerrie's halting but continuous progress through the fantasy and survival, and into the mastery stages of teaching will be explored in the chapters that follow. In saying this, however, a word of caution is in order. There is a tendency among those who use stages as a means for thinking about human development — and among their readers — to reify the stages, that is, to assume they are actual things with clearly discernible boundaries. Nothing could be further from the truth. Human development defies easy categorization. It is seldom smooth, never conflict free, and frequently characterized by backsliding. Such is the story of Kerrie's first year of teaching, just as it is the story of other first-year teachers.

QUESTIONS FOR CONSIDERATION

1. Are your reasons for entering teaching similar to or different from Kerrie's? Do you share a similar set of teaching values — wanting a warm, fun classroom — or a different view?
2. Are your values likely to fit well within an institutionalized teacher role, or will you have some difficulty fitting in?
3. Is the teacher a "ruler" in a kingdom? If not, what are the teacher's role and responsibilities? What is your personal teaching fantasy?
4. Is the context within which Kerrie worked typical? Are you surprised or troubled by any of the work conditions she faced?
5. As a student, were you ever aware of your ability to influence teachers' behavior? How did you put pressure on your teachers to conform to your expectations? How did your teachers respond?

ACTIVITIES

1. Interview a teacher about the quality of his or her work environment. What does he or she like about teaching? What is troubling and why? What aspects of the environment does the teacher control? What areas are there over which he or she has little control?
2. If you have not done so recently, visit a public school and spend a day there. Is it a comfortable place to be? Do you enjoy the students? While in the school ask permission to observe a classroom. Again, is it a comfortable place to be? If not, why not?

2 Planning a Fantasy

How does one go about planning an appropriate educational program before meeting the students, before making any friends on the school staff, or without having had sufficient time to review a wide range of the instructional materials available? This is the problem, with all its uncertainty, that greets first-year teachers — little wonder that they engage in flights of fantasy.

Never having taught junior high age students before (Kerrie student taught in a suburban senior high school), Kerrie sought information useful for planning wherever she could find it. Intellectually, her task was to create a plausible scenario of what the first few weeks of classes would be like — a mental model of the classroom — including what she and her students would be doing and when, and how they would respond. The reasonableness of a scenario is dependent on the kind and quality of information the beginning teacher is able to organize and internalize about students and about the kinds of learning activities and teaching strategies suited to them. In addition, it is dependent on the teacher's ability to conceptualize sensible instructional aims. Inevitably the scenario created represents a simplified model of the classroom, but it does provide a framework within which to work. Clark and Yinger, in their excellent survey of the research on teacher planning (1987), note that one promising avenue for understanding what teachers do is the research on human information processing. They state that "a person, when faced with a complex situation, creates a simplified model of that situation and then behaves rationally in relation to that simplified model." This is precisely what Kerrie did through forming her classroom scenario. We shall begin this chapter by considering how Kerrie went about gaining insight into what seventh graders were like and what they knew.

LEVEL OF INSTRUCTION

To fill out the student portion of the picture, Kerrie (a seventh grader herself, some years before) drew upon her experience as a mother, even though her children were younger, one in fifth grade and the other in sixth: They are "naive, shy, know-it-all brats! (laughter)." *How did she come to this knowledge?* "From my children, I guess. Not that they're the wonder kids or anything. But, they're kids. I have thought about their friends, too. For instance, I've even said, 'do you know if I write ETC., what that means? They said, 'yes, et cetera. Like more and more.'" And she also tried to remember what she was like at that age:

> All I can do is put myself in their place. That's the best I can do because I see my children in the same mold I was in, too. I don't see anything radically different. They know a lot about some things, nothing about other things. You have to give them credit for knowing what they know.

But she realized these were inadequate sources of knowledge and felt insecure. When questioned, she admitted she really did not know what a seventh grader was: "I don't know . . . I don't know." And she worried that her plans would miss the mark. "Maybe I've written my lesson plans for the fifth grade. I wonder."

She gained security by relying on what other teachers had determined were appropriate activities for seventh-grade students and how long such activities would take. She may not have known who these young people were, but surely other teachers could be counted on to know. And so,

> I went [into the school] and said, "Where do I start?" The curriculum was pretty much just handed to me. I am going to teach someone else's social studies unit which was written for the seventh grade. It's not mine. But it looks good to me and I'm going to teach it, at least for my first unit. That's three weeks. After that I'll throw my hands in the air and try and brace for it.

Similarly, she agreed with the other teachers in the team to have learning centers in the language arts area where students would "spend maybe two or three days [on an activity] and then switch. They rotate, so after three weeks or so they've done all the centers." Activities of this kind intuitively seemed appropriate to her. She was certain she did not want to lecture:

> I lectured way too much in my student teaching (sophomores). That was almost all I did. I think I did that because I got a lot of lecturing (as a student). Personally, I liked it. That's great for me. But that doesn't mean

it's great for everybody. So, here I am in seventh grade. I can't lecture to these kids.

She felt a little more confident in the reading area because of her experience reading to her own children:

Someone handed me a seventh-grade reading book. It had great stories in it. I looked at my own children and thought, they're above average, they could handle this. One of my children is a fifth grader and the other is a sixth grader. I've been reading them a seventh-grade book. They're handling it okay. So, it seems to be pretty much right on. Then, I've gone through my own repertoire of short stories and things, and selected things that seem on that same level.

GOALS

While planning for the first few weeks of teaching, Kerrie thought little about instructional goals. In English, objectives were contained in the required textbook. But even in social studies, where she enjoyed a great deal of autonomy, she thought little about goals. Apparently, Kerrie did not consider the establishment of goals a central part of teaching, although selecting activities and organizing materials was. For the most part, goals were to be set elsewhere. She commented, for example, that she did not "see [other] teachers writing down goals." And she was "not getting paid any money to do it." There were only two instances where she thought goal writing necessary: She would write them when required to do so by the principal and when something was obviously in need of change. Otherwise, like the experienced teachers studied by McCutcheon (1982), she intended to put little energy into identifying goals — instructional goals were "unspoken," implicit in the activities and content selected, and "in the head."

When asked what were the goals implicit in the activities she initially had planned, the values of Kerrie's teacher–mother role identity were evident. Her primary concern was with the quality of relations that would exist within the classroom and with the learning climate, rather than with specifically what the students would be learning. For example, she imagined her classroom this way: "Every person is doing what they're supposed to be doing . . . they're interacting with each other and they're having fun. They're being noisy. But it's not boisterous. Everyone is busy and I'm sitting there watching them because I've got them all trained so well." What she hoped for more than anything else was for everyone in the class to "be happy," part of which meant that the students would "do the work well."

DISCIPLINE

An additional element came into play during this stage of planning. The dark side of the fantasy stage brought with it a variety of concerns that shaped how Kerrie thought about planning: "Probably my biggest concern with kids is — that nightmare — they will thumb their noses. 'Do what you want, we're having a party today!'" Concerns of this kind, fear about not being able to control the class, strengthened her initial tendency toward minimizing instructional risks. The message had gotten out to Kerrie that in the beginning the wise teacher is tough and conservative, two qualities that ran counter to her self-image and that proved later to be a source of considerable inner tension as she struggled to come to terms with her authority within the classroom, a problem common to beginning teachers.

> I plan on being as hard as nails the first short while so they feel I'm in control. No one came up to me and said those words. But I've known for years that is a general piece of advice people give to new teachers. But for the most part I have to have an easygoing group, that's how I am.

PLANNING

Kerrie planned in this way in anticipation of the first few weeks of school: She met with the teacher leader from whom she received books and other materials used in the past. After reviewing what had been done, and finding it mostly to her liking, she decided that during the first few weeks of school she would generally follow the schedule of activities established by the team leader, while adding a few personal embellishments wherever possible. In the quiet of her home she then sat down to do her actual planning. Like experienced teachers, she began by thinking about activities and the flow of activities (May, 1986).

> The first thing I do is get out a big calendar. I'm a very calendar-oriented person. A plan book. I block out how much time I want [to cover]. Take a look at the social studies unit, for example. [I said to myself], this ought to cover about three weeks. Block out three weeks. *How do you know it will take three weeks?* It just looks like that much material. I guessed. *So, you blocked out three weeks.* This is the hardest part, to say how long I

want them to spend on it. My guess is—I haven't planned anything beyond these three weeks because I didn't know how long it would take. I figured, OK, a day doing this. Two days doing this, [and it adds up to] three weeks. I don't have anything planned for unit two because I want to see how long unit one takes. How that goes. So, that took care of three weeks right off the bat in social studies. Then, we decided we'd start reading little short stories. So, there are five elements in short stories. One week of review. There's six weeks. So, I planned six weeks just like that!

Kerrie planned by the seat of her pants. She necessarily depended on other teachers' advice, guessed about the length of time various activities would take, and imagined what her students would be like: "I pretty much wrote [my lesson plans] for what I thought was just seventh grade. That's how I'm going to teach it." She would find out whether or not her initial decisions were reasonable and whether or not her view of herself as teacher was accurate only by teaching. There was no other test of the pudding.

In the days prior to the beginning of the school year, and following the completion of her plans, she reviewed mentally what she would do and say in each class period. On the way to school on the first day, this review process continued, similar to running and rerunning a tape of a sequence of events already past.

OPENING OF SCHOOL

The first few days of actual teaching were euphoric: "All I could think about all the way home [after the first day of school] was just that it was as smooth as it could be. Maybe because the kids were intimidated by the first day of school." She took some credit, however, for how well the day went:

> I was prepared, though. I guess I was because it worked out OK. *Why did it go so smoothly?* For one thing, I always go over my lectures—whatever I'm going to say—in my mind. I imagine everybody does that. I always do it 14 times. I guess I just planned well enough. I knew what I was going to say.

Day two also went well, although there were a few problems: "They were bad enough that they got a seating chart today. They wanted to talk so I moved them apart."

Gradually, however, control problems increased. Entire periods were spent "shushing" the students and responding to interruptions while trying to cover the day's content. Even after getting the students quieted down, it would take only a few moments for a low rumble to once again start building; students would turn around in their seats and chat with their neighbors. An occasional student would wander about the classroom and engage a friend. Once in a while a wadded-up piece of paper would sail toward, but seldom go in, the wastepaper basket. Kerrie had not been able to be as "tough as nails": "I walk up and down the aisles and as soon as I've passed them they're back at it again! Chaos before you even blink. As far as you can reach, they're OK. My biggest fear is that pretty soon everyone will know everyone else and I'll have total chaos." A few days later, in near desperation, she said, "I'm not going to live with it, things are going to change. I can't stand it!"

In actuality, while her classes were not orderly, they were clearly not chaotic; it was the fear of chaos more than the reality of a disruptive classroom that appeared to be most troubling to Kerrie. The unsettling question lingering in the back of her mind was whether or not she would win the tug of war with the students over who would control the classroom. She thought she would win, but there were moments of uncertainty when her confidence was shaken.

In response to the situation, her vision of the good classroom seemed to change: "I guess [I want] silence. That must be the key word I want, the thing I want. Maybe that's part of the problem, I don't know exactly what I want." When questioned, she became more clear: "Silence is what I want." But, pausing, she then added, "Not all the time, but at certain times." Kerrie has moved by the third week into the survival stage of teaching.

QUESTIONS FOR CONSIDERATION

1. Kerrie relied heavily on her own children when thinking about and planning for her students. What sources of information will you draw upon, and how will you use them?
2. Have you fantasized about the kind of teacher you will be and about how your students will respond to you? If so, what is your fantasy? What are its origins?
3. Compare and contrast your approach to planning with Kerrie's. What do you do that is similar? Different? Do you begin with a mental scenario of how the class will go? If so, how do you know your scenario is reasonable?

3 A Question of Survival
Planning for Control and Management

For Kerrie the survival stage of teaching came with a flood of grimly insistent problems. Doyle (1986) has observed that "teaching has two major task structures organized around the problems of (a) learning and (b) order. Learning is served by the instructional function [of teachers]. . . . Order is served by the managerial function" (p. 395). Each requires careful planning. Despite a strong emphasis in her teacher education on discipline and management strategies, Kerrie thought comparatively little about the necessity of planning for discipline and management, other than deciding that she would be "tough." Such thoughts were not part of her fantasy. Why she did not plan carefully for management and why her teacher education seemed to have had so little influence on her thinking in this area, despite the widespread concern of beginning teachers with discipline and management issues, is discussed in Appendix B. Suffice it to say that this omission proved to be a source of some of Kerrie's greatest difficulties during the survival stage of teaching. Her explanation for the omission, after realizing it, was remarkable:

I don't know [why I didn't think about it]. I think that I thought that if you planned the curriculum really well, the management just falls into place. I really thought that when I was student teaching. If you are not well planned you are *going* to have problems, but planning well doesn't solve those problems, you still have [management problems]. At first—I'm changing this idea alot—I thought more that you could plan your curriculum and [good] behavior would fall into place; you could handle it as it comes. But you really can't. The other half of planning is what you will require at the same time behaviorally and you can plan for that. Now (sixth month), I plan a lot more things, like transition time and walking into the other room [to check on the students].

So, planning for you is now two kinds of things, but they are not separate. It's like the scenario I've always talked about before. You see it and it's part of the scenario now too. At one time I would see what they were supposed to do; now I know that I also have to tell them what to do so I get that scenario. *You assumed that the students would pick up on what's appropriate behavior for different kinds of activities?* Right. Right. Exactly. It's like you are busy with adults and you do something and then they have a transition and they know how to settle right down. These kids don't know.

It was only when Kerrie was sitting in a management and discipline workshop several weeks into the school year that she fully realized that she needed "to have a game plan" for management: "As I was sitting there it just came to me, I have to have a game plan. So, I started jotting things down." To that point and for a few weeks afterward she struggled with the problem of establishing order within the classroom.

THE PROBLEM

Kerrie had not thought through, in advance of teaching, a number of interrelated management problems:

- What should be done with students who do not complete their work?
- What should be the policy toward late assignments?
- Should she even accept late work?
- What actions should be taken when students misbehave?
- Should she have a "time out" corner somewhere in the room?
- What infraction would result in expulsion from class?
- How should students be moved from one activity into another?
- How should students respond to teacher questions?
- Should they raise their hands, or may they shout out answers?

Unfortunately, the team leader gave Kerrie very little assistance. For example, she did not inform her that there were school policies for dealing with some management problems.

Matters were exacerbated by the presence in her classes of significant numbers of students who behaved in ways outside of her experience; she simply knew very little about these young people, how to respond to them to get them on-task, or what kinds of activities to plan for them, particularly the low-ability group. "I have a boy who should be in resource (a separate program within the school designed for students with relatively severe learning problems). I don't know what to do. He can't find things in the book, let alone get it written down on paper. He can't even get started!" Moreover, in both her low-ability and average groups there were significant numbers of students — very unlike her own children — for whom school seemed to mean little or nothing. There were students like Bart: He attended school infrequently, but when he was there, Kerrie was very much aware of his presence. A tall, pale, boney, long-haired boy who dressed in black, including a black T-shirt with the insignia of a heavy metal band, Bart would sit in class quietly doing nothing. Typically he would just sit, looking about disinterestedly, or occasionally he would wander around the room. Sometimes he would start an assignment at Kerrie's urging, but never complete it, or if he did, he would not bother to turn it in. Bart's silence disturbed Kerrie nearly as much as the noise of some of his classmates. These students had

> No interest in doing well, in completing their jobs without being reminded. For example, I gave this assignment out last Tuesday. Do you know how many people didn't have it done? Five, at least. There were five F's in there! They don't care. They'll just sit there! It surprised me and shocked me.

What Kerrie experienced was a form of culture shock. In response, for a period of time, not knowing quite what to do, she gave into student pressures and lowered her standards, which only increased her frustrations.

There were other troubling students as well:

> There is a girl in here . . . there's one girl who talks very quietly. You [tell her] to speak louder. So, she repeats herself very quietly. I can't stand that! I just want her to scream or . . . something. Ask it nice and loud! Or another girl who just wants to stand by my desk. I just want her to go sit down. She bugs me anyway. A 12-year-old who dyes her hair blonde makes me want to vomit!

The difficulty of keeping these young people on-task, coupled with their frequent expressions of what was to Kerrie, at the beginning of the year, unpredictable and contrary behavior, added up to a major classroom control problem and a concern that she would not be able to handle it adequately. There were brief moments of genuine despair, a sinking feeling: "I have desperate moments. . . . Like this is not going to work, what will I do? That's usually in very noisy times." In contrast, she remarked, "Quiet . . . feels good." Understandably, Kerrie became nearly consumed with establishing control, especially of seventh-period social studies, where she had the greatest influence over the content but the most severe problems:

> [Some] kids want to arm-wrestle or hit. Punch fight. Some things like that. You just can't get them to settle back down. It's too late in the day. The morning kids aren't as bad. It's a smaller class though. Twenty-five kids. Usually the other [core] class [across the pod] is doing what we're doing so I can't say, "Shut up." The other class is being quiet! I feel frustrated.

Internally, a struggle began to take place between Kerrie's desire to maintain her self-identity as a teacher — she still wanted a "fun", warm, "snuggly" class — and her feeling that it was necessary to be a "bitch" in order to achieve the desired levels of control:

> *It was more quiet today, why?* Oh, yes. I decided it would be easier to be a bitch . . . but you can see, I'm still not very good at being hard on them. They know I'm still laughing underneath it. But I have to cope with these kids for nine months. If we're having problems in three weeks it could be chaos [later on]. I just clamped down on them. I finally [decided] I'll send the whole class to the office if I have to. I'm going to be in control!

In addition to feeling she had to be a "bitch," Kerrie was bothered by having to be a policewoman, which was also counter to her teacher's self-image:

> The kids are not as responsible as I had expected them [to be]. I'm a police officer. You know that? I want to just bash their heads together like the Three Stooges, or something! I can't stand it! I can't believe they're not more conscientious than they are!

Having to be a "bitch" and a policewoman made it difficult for her to express herself as she saw herself — a warm, loving, caring, easygoing, teacher–mother — and to establish the kinds of relationships with students that she found most satisfying. "It just drives me crazy that kids can't respond to love. Why can't people respond to someone who shows love in the same way as they respond to someone who shows strictness?" She kicked students out of class — "since the first of October I've just been kicking them right out of class" — but was troubled by doing so.

One effect of this internal struggle was that Kerrie's ability to maintain control and get the students on-task became the central criterion by which she determined her teaching effectiveness. For a brief period of time a "good" day was a day when the students did not misbehave: "What you saw [today], was great . . . I wasn't having big discipline problems. So, that makes it [a good day]. No one was really bugging anyone else in a big way, or bugging the whole class." Days like this renewed Kerrie's confidence: "These kids are really getting whipped into shape!" But good days were followed by "bad" ones, and she vacillated between blaming the students and blaming herself for the problems her classes were having. In her frustration, however, she decided that most of the problems were the students': "I don't know if it's all me, either. It doesn't seem like it should all be me! Sometimes I just think these suckers are lazy! They don't want to understand because it seems way too hard. It's not!" Kerrie's reaction reflects a view widely shared by teachers. Kindsvatter and colleagues (1988), for example, refer to a study conducted by Brophy and Rohrkemper, in which they "found that teachers tend to assign cause to factors outside themselves, often targeting the students directly" when something goes wrong (p. 275).

The need to maintain control also became the central criterion by which instructional decisions were made. Clearly, much was at stake in the success of Kerrie's efforts to gain the respect and compliance of her students. For the sake of increasing control she jettisoned some planned activities. Among the first to go, for example, were the language arts activity centers: Keeping three small groups busy and on-task was much more difficult than keeping one large group working. In addition, she switched the order of planned student activities. For instance, having a quiet group activity rather than independent or small-group work following the return from lunch helped settle the students down and made it easier to get them back on-task. This insight proved to be particularly important as the year progressed.

As the students misbehaved, they inadvertently were pushing Kerrie to give up any idea of planning activities that were fun or a bit risky. The pressure was to conform to the teacher role with which the students were most familiar, even though they saw such a role as resulting in "boring" classes, as was indicated in the student interviews. Control and management problems heightened whenever Kerrie had them engage in activities that were slightly out of the ordinary. For example, an assignment to write an imaginary journal of the pioneer trek across America proved to be an invitation for many students to misbehave: "Sometimes I think up the most simple thing I can possibly think up and they are totally baffled. I mean, I go over these things [and they say], 'Do what?! Write a journal?' Things that should be so simple . . . they make so hard." The temptation was to stop including such assignments in the curriculum at all. "It's like, [teachers have the students] do [the same] things over and over and over again because [the students] know how to do them." But to give up on such activities, ultimately, was to give up a part of herself and to discard much of what she valued most about teaching, and this she could not do.

> I'm not unhappy [with how the students have done with the journal]. I'm not thrilled. But I'd do it again. Sometimes I think, why don't I just have them read [the material] or give a lecture and ask some questions. Well, this is some variety—we've done that other stuff before, this is new.

THE GAME PLAN

As noted, while Kerrie was struggling with these problems she realized she would need a "game plan" if she was to adequately resolve them. The plan that eventually emerged had three parts: First, Kerrie knew that she needed to identify and consistently reinforce a set of classroom rules. There was nothing new in this idea; she had established some general rules beginning on the first day. The problem was that she had not consistently enforced or successfully reinforced them. This problem was tied to her not yet having identified a set of management strategies, including incentives and punishments, by which to obtain and maintain desirable student behavior. Second, she realized that she would have to routinize or systematize many classroom activities if her classes were to be orderly and purposeful. Third, she realized she would have to do a better job of identifying appropriate activities and content to increase student attentiveness.

These three elements of Kerrie's management plan did not suddenly emerge complete with labels and solutions attached to them. Rather, the plan itself needs to be understood in terms of the halting experimentation that characterized Kerrie's attempt to work through the problems of the survival stage of teaching. It was through trial and error, coupled with moments of genuine insight, and in response to specific problems, that this plan emerged. Despite the force with which the initial idea came to her that she would have to have a "game plan," it emerged only gradually. Moreover, even after she had settled on a plan, implementing it several weeks into the term, after the students had already developed habitual ways of responding in class, proved to be very difficult and time consuming: "I'm trying to get [the students into management routines] now, but they're really slow to do it because I've waited [so long]."

The difficulty of making changes after initial patterns of behavior are set is underscored by Clark and Yinger (1987):

Studies of the first weeks of school . . . support the conclusion that, to a significant degree, the 'problem space' . . . within which teacher and students operate is defined early, changes little during the course of the school year, and exerts a powerful, if subtle, influence on thought and behavior. (p. 347)

Consistency, Rewards, and Punishments

While Kerrie had established some general rules of good student behavior, she had trouble sticking to them. Part of the difficulty lay in the persistence of her internal struggle; she had not fully answered the question of what kind of teacher-authority she would be and whether or not she could be that kind of teacher in Rocky Mountain Junior High School. She waffled and behaved inconsistently. As a result, the students received mixed messages, which initially increased the difficulty of managing the classroom and maintaining control: "It's like there aren't any rules and you have to make some up as you go." Kerrie would, for example, introduce a discipline strategy or a form of punishment and change it shortly thereafter. Moreover, she would try a strategy used by the team leader that would seem to encourage the students to behave as she desired, only to discard it upon discovering that it was personally distasteful or contrary to her teaching values. "There are a lot of things that I'd like to do that I can see are very beneficial but that just bother me too much."

She could not depend on the team leader's or other teachers' suggestions uncritically, realizing that they reflected teaching values and classes often quite different from her own. This was a frustrating time, a time of uncertain experimentation: "That's my biggest problem . . . starting out with one idea and still having that idea when I get to the end."

Consistency became possible for Kerrie only once she had tested and found a cluster of rules and some strategies to maintain them with which she could live. Some of these she created herself; others she was able to borrow and still maintain her teaching values. Drawing on her experience as a mother, she realized that treats would likely encourage good behavior, so she brought a large glass cookie jar from home filled with candy and gum and placed it prominently on her desk in the front of the room. She then announced that the treats would be given only to students who demonstrated exceptionally good behavior. The bribe had an immediate and positive effect on classroom behavior. In addition, she set up a contest in reading: those students who read the most books during the year would be taken out for pizza. In the short run, this too encouraged more on-task behavior. One strategy proved to be very troublesome: Kerrie told the students that if they completed their work promptly they could have the remaining time to read quietly. To them, this was an invitation to use the time however they wished, which had unfortunate results for classroom control.

From the team leader she borrowed the strategy of keeping the students in class during breaks a second for every second of time they wasted: "I say, 'hey guys, settle down,' then as soon as I have trouble I'll come up [to the front of the room] and start counting minutes off the clock." When consistently applied, this proved to be an extremely effective tool. She was pleased that it worked so effectively, but irritated that she had found out about it only accidentally when observing through the open area joining the classrooms: "It's really frustrating. Why didn't I know about that? I could have been doing it or using it!"

From the school she initially and unhappily adopted a form of Assertive Discipline (see Canter, 1977), only to discover she was unable to use it effectively. Later, she modified it into a more workable system, but dropped it entirely in her second year of teaching. She also adopted the school VIP (very important person) program. VIP cards were issued to students for good behavior, and each recipient's name was read over the loud speaker to the entire school and was flashed across an electronic announcement board that hung from the ceiling near the office. In addition, each recipient received a school VIP pencil. Oddly, Kerrie found out about the VIP program only by hearing a long list of student names being read over the intercom and then asking what they had done that was so meritorious. Initially, she rather indiscriminately awarded VIPs for silence, but gradually other desirable learning behaviors were included as well.

By nature, Kerrie was not a punitive person. "I hate it," she said, "when I have to be mean." Nevertheless, she found it necessary to identify and implement a few punishments in addition to counting time. As part of the assertive discipline program, after issuing multiple warnings, she isolated misbehaving students at a table set in a corner, or in cases of extreme misbehavior filled out a referral card, which resulted in the student being sent immediately to the office. She also threatened to lower citizenship report card marks.

Getting the incentives and punishments right, and then consistently applying them over time, made a great deal of difference to the quality of Kerrie's classes. She delightedly remarked during one interview early in the school year, for example, that she had had five "good" days in a row. The reason: It "partially comes from [having them] stay after class if we have to, from those little red gum balls, and from the VIPs." Not all went well, however. Just as she would begin to think smooth sailing was ahead, a lesson would fall apart as the students continued, although less energetically, to resist her efforts to socialize them. For example, as the students began to respond to the strategy of keeping them after class if they wasted "her time," a new problem emerged. Following an intolerable increase in noise in one class, she matter of factly commented, "You guys now owe me 30 seconds after school, remind your neighbor." Immediately, nearly all of the students turned in an uproar toward their neighbors and shouted energetically, "SHUT UP!" Exasperated, Kerrie then said, "You now owe me a minute." To Kerrie's dismay, this scene was repeated on several occasions.

Routinization

Establishing effective classroom instructional and management routines plays an extremely important part in obtaining and maintaining desirable student behavior. Routines impose a structure on the classroom environment that reduces the number of decisions teachers need to make and makes predictable the timing and sequence of activities as well as student behavior (Clark & Peterson, 1986). When a teacher sets up a routine, the students, if they are well socialized, immediately know what is expected of them and behave accordingly. They know what is appropriate behavior habitually, which allows the teacher to maintain the flow of the class. But, recall, Kerrie's students were relatively unsophisticated. Among the ways in which their lack of sophistication expressed itself was the limited range of routines they recognized and responded to appropriately. This was not, however, the only difficulty. Kerrie, too, was unsophisticated. The one instructional routine she knew well—lecture and note-taking—she necessarily and rightly rejected as of limited value to the students. She, too, had to learn about routines.

Cautiously venturing out of and beyond the instructional program given to her at the beginning of the year, Kerrie began to identify a loose collection of strategies and classroom activities, and a set of instructional and management patterns by which to organize them, that was more fitting for her and her students. These formed the rudiments of what would eventually become, as her teaching skills improved, a recognizable and defensible teaching style. These included routines for beginning and ending class, doing seat work, correcting papers, taking tests, turning in assignments, as well as for large- and small-group activity.

Identifying Appropriate Content and Activities

Initially, Kerrie relied heavily on the team leader for her curriculum and for methods of teaching it. She found, however, that she could not depend on the team leader's or other teachers' suggestions uncritically, realizing that they reflected teaching values and classes often quite different from her own. This insight was a product of numerous disappointments, of lessons that fell far short of her expectations, sometimes because of lack of skill or knowledge, or because they were inappropriate for the students. For instance, following one such lesson Kerrie commented that she "read to them from the book. Now, that is a bad book [for my students]. It's hard to read. Why I *ever* thought I should do that is beyond me. *Why did you do it then?* Well, [the team leader] suggested it and I thought it must work, so I did it." Feeling insecure, she had chosen not to "make comments about curriculum" in team meetings. She felt bad about her silence, even while adopting the team leader's suggestions and accepting much of the blame if a lesson went poorly. This, too, reflected the internal struggle that was taking place. She wondered aloud, "Why shouldn't I say right out, 'How are you going to teach this? OK, I'll teach this my way and you teach it your way'?"

The problem with rejecting portions of an inherited curriculum is that they must be replaced by something better. Through trial and error Kerrie sought instructional strategies and activities that "worked." A good activity, one that "worked," was one that resulted in the students behaving in the way she imagined they would while planning: "It went as you expected. You saw a scenario and it went that way. So, that's good." As she got to know the students better Kerrie realized, however, that the scenario she had been projecting onto the classroom and around which she had planned was not necessarily fitting. She realized this was a problem before she could do much about it: "If things aren't going the way they're supposed to (as I imagined them), then maybe . . . maybe that's why I'm so upset with [the kids], because they are not [acting in accordance with] this scenario. Maybe they're just normal and I'm weird!"

As Kerrie's knowledge of herself and of her students increased, she became increasingly successful at identifying appropriate content and identifying or creating fitting activities. By mid-year she had recreated much of the inherited curriculum in her own image and that of her students. The teachers studied by McCutcheon (1982) engaged in a similar transformative process.

> If differences between the teacher's style and the role prescribed in teachers' editions [of textbooks] are apparent, somehow teachers must

mentally edit out most of those differences to make the textbooks and the suggestions in teachers' guides fit personal teaching styles and beliefs. Teachers may do this editing consciously or may be almost unaware of it. (p. 268)

Kerrie found, for example, that the students loved to be read to, and she did so with them gathered around her: "Sometimes they'll want to read a novel. It's like reading bedtime stories to your children. It's a warm, fuzzy feeling. Like it could be raining and thundering outside. So, that's a nice, rewarding, quiet time. It's just nice." And so she set aside a certain time every day in reading to read to her students. They loved games, and these, too, were built into the curriculum. For example, she created a trivial pursuit game as a means for reviewing some material they were required to know: "I'm really excited about it. If they don't love it, I'm going to kill them! (laughter). It's all the things they've studied and I think it will be fun for them."

TRANSITION INTO THE MASTERY STAGE OF TEACHING

Once Kerrie established a firm plan of action, and stuck to it long enough for the students to respond, some remarkable changes began to take place. She began to feel much more powerful in the classroom. Just prior to the Thanksgiving holiday, for example, she succeeded in preventing a feared and perhaps fanciful student rebellion—a remnant of the dark side of the fantasy stage of teaching—from materializing: "You don't see rebellion arise in one day. You see it growing over two weeks. As you see that, you adjust and you never get to that point." Part of her success came from becoming much more skilled at pacing her classes and at making transitions from one activity to another. (This will be discussed in greater depth in the next chapter.) She also found that she could overpower the students if necessary and force compliance without doing too much violence to her self-image. Although she could not be a "bitch," she could be tough if she had to be, for the students' own good; still, she preferred not to be. As she put it to the students: "The bottom line is, you're going to have to do this anyway, you might as well do it under a nice feeling in our class [rather than] a Gestapo feeling. But, there are times when the Gestapo is here!" She could also manipulate the students if necessary: "More and more I'm finding I have to manipulate them. Like, I'll stand here and wait for you. Do you want to be quiet so I can give you something or do you just want to sit here until the bell rings and stay after school?"

Her confidence increased with each success. With greater confidence, she reasserted some of the values that initially prompted her to become a teacher and once again became very responsive to the students. Sometimes perhaps she was a bit too responsive and then she reaped the rewards that come with inconsistency:

> I want to treat them as individuals. They're little humans. I respond more to their individual needs. I say, this is what I'll do and they'll just have to toe the line. Then, someone comes up and has a problem. OK, that's reasonable [and I make an exception].

Success also brought with it an increased inclination to be constructively self-critical: "Now, when I look back at some of the things I've done with them, it's pretty scary — the things that they were expected to do [but really couldn't]." There is, of course, a knowledge and a skill dimension reflected in her disposition to be self-critical — she knew something more about the range of options from which she could choose and she felt she had begun developing the skill to organize these activities so that the students would engage them appropriately and well.

PLANNING: THE MASTERY STAGE

Other changes took place in how Kerrie thought about and planned her classes that mark the illusive boundary separating the survival from the mastery stage of teaching. A critical change came when she stopped using her own children as the principal lens through which she viewed her students and began using the students themselves in this way. Although from time to time, even into the second year of teaching, she would occasionally think about her own children when planning an activity or would talk over an idea with them, their importance clearly diminished dramatically. She noted this change herself: "I used to rely more on my children [in planning] than I need to now."

In addition to this shift in focus, five additional significant changes took place, marking Kerrie's move out of the survival stage of teaching:

1. She began planning in greater detail in anticipation of management-related problems.
2. She became much more efficient as a planner.
3. Control was replaced by student learning as the central issue in planning activities.
4. Rather than being primarily concerned with the general questions

of what to do in the classroom and how to do it, Kerrie became more concerned with making refinements and improvements in what she was going to do and how she was going to do it.

5. Feeling she knew her students' and her own interests and abilities well, she planned with much greater certainty; she became less of an "impulsive consumer" (May, 1986, p. 9).

Greater Detail and Better Anticipation

Kerrie continued to begin planning by filling out a "big calendar," as she had done since the fantasy stage of teaching. She continued to block out the amount of time she thought it would take to cover a chapter or complete a given activity, but she added another level to her planning, a refinement. Kerrie began to write detailed notes to herself on 3M Post-it Note Pads, which she would stick on the calendar or on an assignment. These notes contained specific reminders of things to do that she might otherwise forget, particularly relating to maintaining the flow of the lesson:

> I do more lesson plans. But they look kind of funny in my book because lots of times I'll use one of those sticky papers and stick it on top of the assignment . . . like tomorrow we are going to play a game . . . when the time comes [for me to begin the game] I might get flustered and set it up wrong. [To prevent that] I now tend to write things down . . . like "choose an umpire," "write their names on the board." Just little things like that that help me.

Planning carefully and well, as Good and Brophy (1987) note, has a profound effect on student behavior. Being prepared — having the room set up appropriately and the materials ready; being aware of likely spots where students might become confused; in short, attending to all the details possible — increases the likelihood that the teacher will be able to establish and maintain a brisk, purposeful lesson flow that minimizes student misbehavior.

The notes Kerrie wrote to herself were a reflection of an internal, ongoing conversation she began to have about planning. In effect, planning became a part of life, something she was doing continually even while standing in front of a class instructing.[1] As ideas would pop into

---

[1] Clark and Yinger (1987), drawing on the work of Schon, describe "reflective conservation" about practice as one of the characteristic activities of "design" professionals, those whose work involves "action aimed at bringing about desired states of affairs in practical contents" (p. 360).

her head, as she ran across a useful item, or as she thought of something she needed to attend to more carefully, she would expand her notes and revise her plans, sometimes on the spot. In this way Kerrie not only became better organized but also was better able to monitor her own behavior to make certain that activities flowed as intended and to anticipate problems. A few days before she was to teach a lesson, she reviewed her calendar to recall what activities she had planned and in what sequence, read her notes, and then gathered the necessary materials. She would again review her plans just prior to teaching to refresh her mental image of what was to transpire. The teachers studied by McCutcheon (1982) planned in a similar way. However, it appears as though the notes they wrote to themselves were more content related than management related. Near the end of this study, Kerrie wrote fewer notes to herself and they, too, tended to be more concerned with content.

Kerrie also altered the way in which she approached the content to be taught. Initially, she focused almost exclusively on student activities — what they would be doing with the content — rather than on the content itself. For example, hoping to save some time, which was at a premium, she had not carefully read the texts she was using, believing that as a college educated person she knew her material and that she could trust those who wrote the texts. What she discovered was that she had to pay much closer attention to the relationship between content and learning activity. Without attending carefully to what the students were reading, she was unable to effectively anticipate areas where problems might occur, nor was she able to rearrange the material into a more appropriate order for her students. In addition, even the slightest teacher confusion or uncertainty disrupted the lesson's momentum and increased the likelihood of misbehavior. Effective managers know their content thoroughly and well (Good & Brophy, 1987).

Kerrie's attitude was replaced by another:

[Unlike with this unit,] I am teaching the next unit. I *am* taking it home. I *am* reading the book. I haven't even read the chapter I'm teaching [in this unit]. I know it (the content), but I haven't read it. [Because of that, I haven't been able to teach the material as I'd like.] I'm changing [the next unit] around. I'm going to teach it my way rather than just [follow what's there].

And later:

It took me about three times of starting it (the assigned book) and I finally thought, I have to sit down and read this all together and answer these questions as I go, in order to get focused on what was happening.

It was Kerrie's "sixth sense," as she called it, that allowed her to plan with greater anticipation: She became better able to predict how students would respond to different kinds of activities and to anticipate potential problem areas. For instance, she became better able to predict accurately how long it would take the students to complete assignments. "I'll look at the whole book and see how far I want to get. Divide it into sections and decide how much time to spend on each thing and organize activities or the lectures." *How do you know how long it will take?* "It is my sixth sense."

In addition, Kerrie "overplanned," which had a profound effect on classroom management:

> I overplan now. *And you didn't before?* No, and that got me into trouble, it left me open to problems. [Now] I'd rather bombard them than let them bombard me with their free time. They say to me all the time, "Why do you give us this book, and this back-of-the-book exercise and this worksheet?" And I say, "When you're through with that come and get this." In other words "Stay busy!" Instead of just saying, just do this page and then you're free to wreak havoc all over the place when you're through, it says to them that I'm expecting them to be busy all of the time, and that's much easier on me. *That is a change!* Yes.

Increased Efficiency

Kerrie became a more efficient planner. As she got to know her students better she became better able to plan appropriate activities and sequences of activities, with the result that there was a great deal less class time wasted and less disruptive behavior. She became more skilled at the actual process of planning, of simultaneously attending to and simplifying the demands of "content, standardized curriculum expectations, available resources and materials, and . . . pupils' interests and abilities" in the attempt to produce appropriate lessons (May, 1986, p. 8). In this process, simplification is of great importance—no one can attend to all that is actually involved in planning, no one can possibly satisfy every demand or anticipate every problem. Kerrie became, for example, better able to separate important from comparatively less important demands. She also simplified by becoming more consistent, as previously noted. For instance, she became less willing to make exceptions, which only complicated her work: "I've just flat out said no. You could have studied [but you didn't]. If they don't have [the work done] by Friday, they're never going to bother anyway." And she learned how to use her planning time more effectively: "I'm learning how to plan during my planning period. Doesn't that sound funny?"

Displacement of Control

As Kerrie moved into the mastery stage of teaching, control was displaced by student learning as the primary concern of planning. This was a subtle shift, in part because classroom control continued to be very important. During the early part of the survival stage, Kerrie thought about activities with the expectation of maintaining silence. Later, this changed: "OK, I [used to plan] an activity for seventh period and I [would expect] silence. [Now,] I will say, 'This is the activity, how much silence should I expect?'" Moreover, once again a "good" day became more than a day when the students did not misbehave; it was a time when "things go as planned and go beyond what is planned . . . seeing [the students] go ahead and do [the work]." Days like this, which reflected a change in priorities, brought feelings of euphoria:

> I went to lunch today and said, "This is the best day I've ever had in my life!" I feel that quite often. Gee, I have really fun things for them [to do]. They're on it, they're on-task and they're understanding it . . . and they like school! My morning kids like school!

Making Refinements

Planning became more a matter of making refinements in an acceptable program of activity than of establishing the program itself. One indication of this change was that the nature of the occasional questions she asked other teachers changed somewhat. Rather than asking what to teach, as she did at the beginning of the year, she asked detailed instructional and curriculum questions: "Knowing what points to cover is usually what I'm aiming at. Covering certain points. For example, the due date: What should be included? If [the students] can work with other [students]. If [the students] could use a free assignment pass on this. Just a whole variety of items that would need to be told to the kids." Another indication was that Kerrie's planning came to be characterized by controlled flexibility. She knew generally what kinds of activities were most appropriate for herself and her students and generally how to organize them. As a result she no longer found it necessary to swing dramatically between different types of activities in the hope of landing on one that worked; nor, at the other extreme, did she need to hold tightly to the team leader's program. Rather, somewhat like rearranging flowers, she had identified a cluster of activities around which she moved in response to changes in the teaching context in order to achieve the desired learning result: "Sometimes I'll look ahead during the week and decide to switch, like today's lesson with Friday's, maybe because of the mood the kids are in or the kind of day it is. Sometimes there is a day when the kids are just crazy. They can't do certain things or they need something." In this way she could keep the students on-task and learning, and she could minimize misbehavior, which was essential to her own feelings of self-worth.

Greater Confidence

Finally, Kerrie planned with much greater confidence and certainty. She became much less willing to include activities in her plans just because the activities were part of the team leader's program. "I'm more self-assured," she said, "and I don't feel like I'm running for help. I feel more like I'm asking to share [other teachers'] ideas." When she did adopt an idea, she adapted it to her own style and to her students: "Very often I'll adapt [others' ideas] to my own way." And later, "I definitely adapt everything to myself." A related factor that helped build her confidence was her growing recognition of the strengths and weaknesses of other teachers who, she noticed, also had management problems and that by comparison she was not doing too badly.

> I still compare myself to other teachers. Sometimes you think—when your class is noisy—you think other teachers never have a class this noisy. Now, sometimes my class is quiet and other classes are noisy . . . yes, they're pretty noisy sometimes . . . so, I'm feeling more equal. Maybe I'm just feeling more secure, too.

She spoke up more in team meetings and felt comfortable breaking stride with other team members: "[The team leader] will probably mention [the explorers] for a couple of days. I'm going longer than that." And, as noted earlier, she became more openly self-critical and also forward looking:

> I look back and I think, what a waste of three weeks in social studies. I don't even like the way it began. I don't like the unit very well. There are so many things I can include. Now . . . next year it will be wonderful! Think of what it will be like in five years! (laughter).

CONCLUSION

The onset of threatening control and management problems jolted Kerrie out of the fantasy stage and into the survival stage of teaching. To conclude this chapter, we will briefly consider a few of the ways in which Kerrie was both helped and hindered in her struggle to come to terms with these problems by the work context of Rocky Mountain Junior High School as well as by her own personal qualities and values.

Throughout the survival stage, Kerrie maintained her self-confidence, more or less. To be sure, it was battered, but it endured even during the most difficult times, times when, as she put it, "you remember the negative and forget the good." At such times, she propped up her sagging confidence with sheer dogged determination; she would not fail! As she moved through the survival stage of teaching, the nature and grounding of her confidence changed, however. The naive confidence of the fantasy stage dissolved, to be replaced by confidence arising from having succeeded in a genuine test of her mettle.

Entering the classroom for the first time with the belief that her students would be like her own children, and like she was as a seventh grader, and would be interested in learning and responsive to teaching through love, undoubtedly contributed to Kerrie's initial management and control problems. Clearly, she did not anticipate having to deal with the level of misbehavior and disinterest that met her. She was surprised and a bit dismayed by this discovery, which presented a challenge to some of her most fundamental teaching values. Would the students allow her to be the fun-loving, nurturing teacher she had hoped to be? This question was in doubt almost to mid-year. Eventually, however, she found a more or less satisfying middle ground between the "bitch" she detested and the wishy-washy and undemanding teacher she disdained. The process of negotiation that produced this compromise, however, was difficult. What she discovered was that the road to a fun, warm, "cuddly" classroom sometimes went directly through the police station: Even for her, there were no detours allowed.

One way of understanding Kerrie's dilemma is in terms of the different kinds of power that may be drawn upon by teachers in order to gain and maintain control. Five types have been identified by researchers:

1. Referent, which is based on the teacher's personality
2. Expert, which is tied to the teacher's knowledge
3. Legitimate, which is a reflection of the teacher's position as teacher
4. Coercive, which flows from a teacher's ability to punish
5. Reward.

Of these, "referent power has the greatest impact on cognitive and affective learning, but expert power also has a favorable effect. Legitimate power and coercive power tend to retard both aspects of learning" (Kindsvatter, et al., 1988, pp. 275–76). Kerrie entered the classroom expecting students to behave because of who she was, a caring fun-loving nurturer. They did not, however, respond as she had expected based on her student teaching experience. Thus, her frustration: "It just drives me crazy that kids can't respond to love!" In response, and unhappily, to gain control she invoked power drawn from rewards and occasional coercion, while continuing to struggle to express herself in the classroom and with the students as she saw herself. Judicious use of coercion and rewards helped her gain a measure of control, which eventually made it possible to build caring relationships with an increasingly larger number of students. As she built caring relationships — as the students and she got to know each other better — her referent power grew until it was the dominant source of Kerrie's power within the classroom: In this way, Kerrie got to be Kerrie in the classroom.

As a loner, Kerrie generally resisted going to other teachers for help with her management and control problems. Maybe the team leader sensed this quality in Kerrie and for this reason maintained her distance throughout much of the year, only warming up to Kerrie near year's end. Kerrie's tendency to withdraw into herself and to deal with problems essentially in isolation made her movement through the survival stage of teaching more difficult than it otherwise might have been. Yet, there was an ambivalence about her feelings. Her view was that while working in Rocky Mountain Junior High School she was generally on her own: "You're on your own, planning wise." Responding to this message, she rarely requested help, perhaps fearing the appearance of weakness, and yet she wanted and needed it. Simultaneously, she enjoyed the feeling of autonomy that came from benign neglect, but at times being neglected and feeling isolated troubled her. Others, she thought, should have offered their assistance without being asked. In particular, she found the behavior of the team leader troubling. Undoubtedly, the strength of the message that teachers, even beginning teachers, must make it on their own, along with the failure of teaming, the heavy work load at Rocky Mountain Junior High, and the high visibility of teaching mistakes (which were very public), all contributed to Kerrie's tendency to withdraw into herself, a tendency she resisted late in the year in order to further her professional growth.

Given the amount and rapid pace of work, Kerrie had very little time to pause to consider the implications of her actions. Instead she, perhaps like most beginning teachers, fell back on long established patterns of belief and action, what one researcher has called a "socialized logic," built over years of observing teachers and of being a parent (Crow, 1987). Common sense reigned supreme until what was common was clearly proven either inadequate or inaccurate. For the most part, however, Kerrie was fortunate because her common sense served her reasonably well, although it was the strength of her common sense, confirmed by her student teaching experience, that made her impervious to the message presented during her teacher education that she would need to plan carefully for discipline and management. Such a view was contrary to her teacher identity, which told her that personality and a fun curriculum would win students over and eliminate control problems. Ultimately, Kerrie's movement into the mastery stage of teaching was dependent on the enhancement of common sense by reason: Only in this way was she able to attack in a consistent and fruitful manner the problems that confronted her. It was in a reflective moment, for example, that the fundamental insight came to Kerrie that in order to gain control of her classes she would need a management game plan.

On the positive side, Rocky Mountain Junior High School presented Kerrie with a curriculum that, although eventually she transformed somewhat, at least offered her a point of departure for her own planning. And, despite his infrequent visits, she knew she had the confidence and trust of the principal, which helped her feel more secure. Moreover, she could observe the team leader teaching through the open area, which proved to be a source of many useful ideas, even though it also produced feelings of their being in competition. And finally, although the students often troubled her, they were wonderfully forgiving of her mistakes and seemed to think more of her as a teacher than she often thought of herself. To them, she was, as one student put it in an interview, "nice and fun." They were even pleased that she was a first-year teacher, because, as another student commented, "it seems like [when teachers have taught for a few years] they're really grouchy and they know how to handle you and everything. She seems easygoing . . . if you have a problem you can go to her and she'll explain it right away."

QUESTIONS FOR CONSIDERATION

1. Describe how you go about planning a vacation or a trip to the supermarket? Do you approach such problems systematically or do you just set out? Do you find it helpful to write down what you wish to accomplish?
2. Think about a recent lesson you taught. How did you think it

through? Did you plan for management as well as instruction? From what sources did you gather ideas? Upon what grounds did you choose to teach one idea rather than another or place one topic before another?

3. Think of a tight spot you recently got yourself into. Did you maintain your self-confidence? Did you successfully work it through? What qualities do you possess that help you get through such times successfully?

4. How do you greet failure? Do you meet it with renewed determination or do you tend to withdraw and get angry and discouraged?

ACTIVITIES

1. Discuss with a teacher you respect the process he or she goes through when planning a lesson or unit. Does the person write his or her plans down? If so, what do they include? If not, why not? As a beginning teacher you should pay particular attention to the way in which problems are anticipated.

2. Review a copy of a local district or state curriculum guide in the content area(s) you will be teaching. Is the guide one you could use easily and comfortably? Does it lend itself to the way in which you plan? Does it include all the areas of study you think should be covered? What is missing and why?

4 Facing the Common Problems of Beginning Teachers

As teachers report them, the problems of teaching have remained quite consistent from the early studies of the 1930s to the present, for both elementary and secondary education teachers. For beginning teachers, although they typically master the problem gradually, classroom discipline is by far the most serious challenge they face (Veenman, 1984). This was certainly the case for Kerrie, as discussed in Chapters 2 and 3. There are, however, additional pressing problems that must be dealt with, and it is these that will be considered in this chapter in relation to the development of a variety of teaching skills. But first a word of caution is in order: While these are common problems, identified by Veenman from his review of 91 studies published since 1960, not all beginning teachers have them. Whether or not they do is the result of the interaction of personal characteristics and the teaching context: The skills, understandings, and attitudes a beginning teacher brings into the classroom as well as the work context itself determine what problems will be faced.

The common problems cited by beginning teachers, according to Veenman (1984), are listed in descending order:

1. Classroom discipline;
2. Motivating students;
3. Dealing with individual differences among students;
4. Assessing students' work;
5. Relationships with parents;
6. Organization of class work;
7. Insufficient materials and supplies;
8. Dealing with problems of individual students.

In total, Veenman lists 24 such problem areas. When surveyed, principals offered a slightly different ordering than beginning teachers, elevating teaching slow learners and "devising schemes of work," for example (p. 158). Happily, not all were problems for Kerrie. Of the teacher-reported items, the first five will be discussed in order, starting with a description of the problem area as Kerrie experienced it (with the exception of classroom discipline) followed by what she did to improve the situation.

CLASSROOM DISCIPLINE

In Chapter 2 Kerrie's difficulties with classroom discipline and management were described, and in Chapter 3 some aspects of how she got a handle on the problem were discussed, primarily as related to planning. Kerrie discovered, the hard way, that "smooth functioning of the classrooms of successful managers results from thorough preparation and organization at the beginning of the year" (Good & Brophy, 1987, p. 220). While it is unnecessary to further describe the problem, it is necessary to note an additional set of specific teaching skills that Kerrie developed that played a very significant role in her gaining an acceptable level of control over her classes. In particular, these are skills related to the prevention of misbehavior.

"With-it-ness"

At the beginning of the year Kerrie was not completely "with it." "With-it-ness" is a concept used by researchers to describe teachers who are fully aware of what is happening in the classroom and who, through continuous monitoring, let the students know that they always know "'what is going on' in their classrooms" (Good & Brophy, 1987, p. 260). Initially Kerrie had some difficulty being "with it," reading the classroom and determining what was actually taking place and how she should respond while instructing. This is an extraordinarily complex skill, in actuality, a cluster of skills, to develop, partly because there is so much that goes on in any classroom at any given moment and partly because it is difficult to determine the meaning of events in terms of the purpose and flow of an activity or a lesson. Being "with it" requires the ability to simultaneously attend to a variety of stimuli and then to appropriately categorize what is observed and quickly respond in a way that will prevent disruption and maintain the flow of the lesson. In making decisions of this kind, context is of great importance. It takes time for the beginning teacher to learn what kinds of student actions are fitting for what kinds of teaching activity.

As the year progressed Kerrie became more "with it"; she started to form the "eyes in the back of her head" that expert teachers possess. Her being "with it" was most obvious during teacher-centered activities such as lecturing and correcting assignments and tests. For example, during one mid-year observation Kerrie stood in the front of the room correcting a social studies assignment on the differences between fact and opinion. Without disrupting the flow of the activity, she occasionally called students' names to remind them to attend and even ordered a disruptive student to move, without a significant loss of lesson momentum: "David, move your body right under the teacher's nose." Similarly, during a spelling bee she occasionally reminded the students, in between giving spelling words, of what was appropriate behavior and reprimanded those who misbehaved: "Stand up, you can never get out of this game!"

Physical Presence

Part of the particular character of a teacher's "with-it-ness" is tied to the physical presence established in the classroom. A teacher's body and voice are disciplinary tools. Kerrie is quite small physically, and she is hardly overpowering. In comparison with the team leader's voice, hers is soft, small — but not weak — gentle, mature, and pleasant. She did not have the voice, nor the inclination, to let her students know she was watching by screaming at them when she caught them misbehaving, although they were occasionally, and unintentionally, assaulted by the team leader's voice ripping across the airways from the other classroom. Though Kerrie was tempted briefly to try to overpower the students with her own voice to remind them who was in charge, she realized before trying that she simply could not, physically, be a screamer. She made the best of the voice she had. Her discovery was that she did not need to yell to be commanding; indeed, a soft voice can be very commanding. Rather than scream at the students when they misbehaved, she gradually learned to "talk to them quietly before they got rowdy." The effectiveness of this approach was underscored during one week very late in the school year when she had a bad case of laryngitis, the bane of a talking profession, and could barely speak in a whisper. One wonders what would have happened to her classes had she been a screamer without a voice! What did happen was that the students were remarkably well behaved and seemed to make a point of not taxing her voice by their acting out. Even in a whisper, she was generally in command of the classes.

Presence is also established by how a teacher moves about the classroom. Often the temptation for beginning teachers is to hide. The first few weeks of the school year Kerrie gave in to this temptation, perhaps remembering how her own teachers behaved. For example, she would finish giving an assignment and go sit at her desk hoping for a moment's peace and expecting the students to get to work. Not yet having mastered the ability to give directions clearly and in anticipation of student problems — also essential skills to the prevention of disruptions — the moment she sat down she was swarmed by students wanting help or seeking clarification. Buzzing around her, they blocked her view of the rest of the class, some of whom took this as an opportunity to disrupt. While she attempted to help those surrounding her, in particular those who most aggressively bludgeoned her with questions, students awaiting assistance chatted noisily (participating in the swarm was one way of visiting with a friend seated across the room), as the general noise level in the classroom crept upward.

The situation rapidly became intolerable: "I'll give instructions and go sit down [at my desk]. Bam! One hundred kids who did not hear me give a single instruction four times or even bother to ask their neighbor [rush up]. It's hard for me to have a checkout lane around the desk." By the third week she decided that the mob scene had to end: "All of a sudden, finally, I said, 'If I see people coming my way, I'll say, raise your hand, I'm coming. Don't come up here.'" From then on Kerrie became much more of a physical presence within the classroom. Usually she moved about the room energetically, seeking signs of confusion or inattention, occasionally presenting a lecture at the same time. Frequently during seat work she moved about swiftly, engaging students who had problems; when the class was working quietly and students were not seeking her assistance, she still periodically circulated the room making certain they were engaged: "It's kind of, you run around and remind them of what they are supposed to be doing." An additional advantage of circulating was that close proximity made it more likely that students who were having difficulties but were unlikely to raise their hands to ask for assistance would obtain the help needed and not disrupt.

As the year progressed, Kerrie continued to monitor her classes in this way: She was everywhere, or so it seemed. There were, however, some subtle changes that took place. Initially, she had some difficulty pacing herself; she would stay overly long with one student while others went unaided, which increased the likelihood of off-task behavior. Gradually, she better learned how to give appropriate clues to nudge a student along without having to stay right at hand. Later in the period she would return to see whether the student was continuing to have difficulty and would offer additional help if needed; some students, she realized, would gladly monopolize all her time, with unfortunate results for class behavior and learning. Additionally, she learned that when beginning a class, her position within the room made a difference in how quickly the students would settle down and get ready for instruction. Rather than begin a class from behind her desk, or wherever she happened to be standing when the buzzer sounded, she stood in the front of the room, signaling that she expected all eyes to be on her so that she could set the stage for the day's work: "Time to be quiet. Turn to page 94." A related change took place: Through monitoring students in this way Kerrie began to recognize common problems. Rather than continuing to deal with them on an individual basis, she would stop the class, note the problem, and attempt to resolve it, which minimized student confusion and the resulting disruptions. And during seat work, when the students were working quietly, she frequently scanned the classroom while sitting in the front of the room on a stool. At the slightest noise she would look up from her work and locate the source of the disruption and deal with it.

Lesson Pacing

Another set of skills Kerrie developed that helped minimize her discipline problems had to do with lesson pacing. Establishing an appropriate pace proved to be a very difficult skill for Kerrie to develop. This is hardly surprising given her limited knowledge of the students and the curriculum at the beginning of the year. Lessons frequently went too quickly, leaving the students time at the end of the period in which to disrupt. Sometimes the pace was too slow, and the students disengaged from the lesson: "It's like the longer you give them, the longer they mess around." The essential condition necessary for Kerrie to resolve her pacing problem, and the discipline problems that arose from it, was an increased understanding of the students.

Several specific skills should be mentioned at this point. Part of establishing an appropriate pace, of establishing and maintaining the flow of a lesson in order to minimize disruptions, is being prepared. As Good and Brophy (1987) note, this is a sign of skilled management: Skilled managers, they observe, seldom have to "interrupt the flow in order to consult the manual to see what to do next or to obtain a prop that should have been prepared earlier, and they seldom [confuse] the students with false starts or backtracking to present information that should have been presented earlier" (p. 220). As Kerrie became more familiar with the curriculum, and prepared more carefully with an eye toward management problems, she was better able to maintain lesson flow and direction; and disruptions became less frequent as a result.

Another part of establishing lesson momentum is to begin class on time. At the beginning of the year Kerrie wasted a good deal of time shushing the students in order to get them to settle down and pay attention, believing that class should not be started until all the students were attending. By year's end, her view had changed, and she started class immediately in order to gain student attention and get the lesson flowing. A typical lesson began this way:

8:36: The bell rings. Kerrie immediately calls "Prepared."

8:37: "OK, we're on page 50. Pay attention, we will have a quiz at the end of the chapter. I expect you to have your books open." She begins reading to them from *The Witch of Blackbird Pond* and they follow. Absolute silence. She occasionally stops to ask a question: "Why would Judith feel bad?" Back to the reading.

Establishing effective transitions between activities is also an extremely important pacing skill. This, too, is an area in which Kerrie made steady progress. At the beginning of the year movement from one activity to another was a signal to the students to misbehave, and they frequently did. Part of her success, as noted previously, came from the gradual identification of a small number of instructional routines that, when internalized, enabled the students to move from one activity into another with minimal disruption of the flow of the lesson. A typical transition (which had been routinized) followed the reading activity noted above (almost every language arts class began the same way, with Kerrie reading to the students). Kerrie stopped reading and immediately said to the class:

OK, take out a piece of paper and write your name on it. I'm going to ask you questions on the first five chapters of the book. Close your books. . . . Last question: What was Kit's reaction when she found out there was a second service in the afternoon? (a brief pause). Put your name on the paper (a second reminder). OK. Exchange papers with a partner.

A technique that helped improve lesson pacing and that Kerrie used effectively — one she noted by observing the team leader teach through the open area connecting the rooms — was to establish a specific time limit for an activity and sometimes count down minutes. "You have ten minutes to do the skills practice [assignment] and then we'll have a

spelling bee." Yet another was to give clues, like she did while monitoring individual seat work, to groups of students to speed up their work
and to increase the likelihood of success. I "kind of run around and give
clues according to how I want [the activity to be going], ideally."

Results

There was no sudden noticeable increase in Kerrie's discipline- and
management-related skills; rather, they evolved as part of her overall
effort to gain and maintain control of her classes and to get the students
learning. Moreover, their effectiveness as primarily preventive measures
can be understood only as part of the initial "game plan" she developed.
As discussed in Chapter 3, that plan included clarifying the rules and
consistently reinforcing them through proper incentives and punishments, establishing routines by which to structure the environment, and
building an appropriate curriculum. One of the interesting develop-
ments that came with her increased ability in these areas, especially
becoming more "with-it," was that she experienced teaching somewhat
differently, likening it to being a conductor: Teaching is "like directing
an orchestra . . . reading the music at the same time [that] you are
listening. Predicting."

MOTIVATING STUDENTS

November 11: Do you know what I want to do? [I want to tell them,]
"Everyone who wants to learn today, stay. Everyone who just wants to
bullshit and mess around, you may go! I don't want you [in class]!" Can
we do that? [No, but] that's what you want to do! Some of the kids are
saying, "sh, sh, sh." They're sitting here waiting [for work to begin]. They
get punished, I get punished [by the students who won't get to work].

With the onset of the survival stage of teaching, Kerrie's discipline
and management problems overwhelmed her concern for student motivation. Her aim was to obtain control, even as she struggled to come to
know the students and to come to grips with the teacher role presented
to her by Rocky Mountain Junior High School. Fortunately for the
students, she realized rather quickly that being in control was closely
related to student motivation. It was at this point, as noted previously,
that a good day became more than a day when the classes were merely
well behaved; it became a day when they learned what Kerrie intended:
A good day is when "things go as planned and go beyond what is

planned. . . . seeing [the students] go ahead and do [the work]." But, moving from this insight to actually having students actively engaged in learning proved to be challenging throughout the year. Indeed, the problem of student motivation is not likely to go away completely, even for expert teachers. So serious is the problem that there is some evidence to suggest that many experienced teachers do not believe students can be motivated! (Brophy & Kher, 1986).

The shift from control as the primary teaching concern to student learning brought with it a subsequent increased concern for student motivation. Kerrie wanted the students not only to be well behaved, but also to be actively engaged in and enjoying learning.

> I've kind of had a turnaround in the last week. I've felt I [haven't been] teaching. I gave a test [and] they failed it. They failed the test. So, I said, "You guys aren't learning . . . I'm unhappy about that. Why aren't you learning?" Because they're not studying, they're not motivated and it's such good stuff! It's really fun. But, they're not getting that. They don't know it's fun.

Brophy and Kher (1986) provide a list of "conditions" for the development of intrinsic motivation to learn. Those conditions are useful for speaking about Kerrie's growth:

> (a) a patient, encouraging teacher who supports students' learning efforts and does not engender anxiety through hypercritical or punitive treatment; (b) an appropriate match between student ability and task difficulty, so that students can expect to succeed if they put forth reasonable effort . . . ; (c) sufficient task quality and appropriateness (the tasks make sense as effective means for accomplishing worthwhile academic objectives); (d) sufficient task variety and interest value to minimize boredom due to sheer satiation; and (e) a generalized teacher tendency to present academic tasks as learning opportunities assisted by a helpful instructor rather than as ordeals to be endured or hurdles to be cleared merely in order to please a demanding authority figure. (p. 261)

In utilizing this list, it is important to note that the focus is on the development of intrinsic, or what Brophy and Kher term "task-endogenous" motivation, rather than extrinsic motivation, which is based on rewards or instrumental value of some kind. But, from their review of the relevant literature, they note that under the pressure of accountability and grading, "task-endogenous" motivation is very rare in schools. They conclude that "there is little evidence of student motivation to learn in the typical classroom" (pp. 282–83). Given this situation, it may be necessary, however unfortunate, for teachers to judiciously use rewards and punishments to obtain student performance, but "they will not develop task-endogenous motivation to learn (except perhaps indirectly)" (pp. 263–64). Kerrie's efforts as they relate to each of the five "conditions" will be discussed. First, however, an additional word is in order: Kerrie's effort to motivate her students should be understood in the light of her attempt to gain control of the classroom, which included the use of rewards and punishments to increase on-task behavior. As noted, the students generally were externally motivated by VIPs and candy. They were also externally motivated, by year's end, by the desire to please Kerrie, a reflection of her increasing reliance on referent power, as mentioned in Chapter 3. Despite this, however, her ideal remained that of encouraging the students to become intrinsically motivated.

Encouragement

Kerrie was a very positive person. She delighted in student progress and was rarely critical of student efforts, although as the year passed she frequently expressed disappointment to those who performed at a level obviously below their ability. She sought to create a classroom that was "like a home," affectively: warm, supportive, caring, but not a womb. As the mother–teacher within the "home," her task included encouraging student learning efforts. She did this in a variety of ways. For example, at mid-year the following exchange—which also serves as another example of being "with-it"—was recorded: In a language arts lesson on singular and plural verbs Kerrie was reading aloud sentences from the book and calling on the students to give the correct form, when suddenly she stopped: "OK, John, you must understand this since you are talking. Do number one and talk about it." The student was baffled. Rather than going on to another student, satisfied that John had been put in his place, Kerrie patiently rephrased the question and worked through the problem with him while the entire class listened silently.

The message sent to John and to the rest of the class was that she expected them to be engaged in the lesson and would help them to do so. As Kounin (1970) has observed, the messages teachers send to students have a "ripple effect" (p. 2). The lesson continued: "Annie, do number two and talk about it." Annie, who was frequently disruptive, was dismayed. Reading her face, Kerrie lowered her anxiety by commenting, "Wow, that's complicated!" and then began to work through the problem with the student. Through what Kerrie said and, more importantly, how she said it, she encouraged the students in this class to engage what is generally considered to be a very uninspiring topic, and they succeeded, with her help.

Match of Tasks to Abilities

Through trial and error, Kerrie gradually came to understand what the students generally could and could not do, and how fast she could move them along, making certain they were succeeding:

> *So, the way that you plan these things is you just plan that the students won't know and hope that they will?* Pretty much. Then I can go faster if they all get or know it already. I do, I plan that they won't know it, that I'm going to have to explain it all in detail. It's just amazing.

To help her obtain a better match between student ability and task difficulty, she began to flesh out a kind of generic image of a seventh grader: "I've slowly gotten to know what things they might and might not know. I can't really say how, except by prior experience through the year." Operationally, this generic seventh grader came to be tied to a "steering group" in Kerrie's classes, "a small subset of a class that [teachers use] as an informal reference group for decisions about pacing a lesson or unit" and about activity selection (Clark & Peterson, 1986, p. 256). Membership in this group changed somewhat throughout the year. By mid-year it was composed of generally good students who did their work and were not disruptive. They included Sally, who was one of four students interviewed for the study and who is briefly described later in this chapter in the section on parents.

Not all was trial and error, however. Kerrie sped up the process of coming to know the students by carefully reviewing tests and assignments to identify problem areas. In the process she became progressively more skilled at identifying activities that were at a desirable level of difficulty — not too hard, but not too easy either:

> I totally dumped that test. It didn't even count. I didn't even average those in when I averaged grades. It was just stupid [to have given it]. It was like a professor coming in and teaching my students. When you've just gotten out of college, that's where you are [mentally]. You really are. You're not thinking [about how seventh graders learn].

She also discarded an assignment because it proved to be impossible for the students to do adequately, and she let them know of the decision.

Wanting her students to feel good about themselves, Kerrie attempted to locate or create activities that would let the students shine. One such opportunity presented itself when it was her team's responsibility to produce the school newspaper:

> We're (the core leader's and my classes) writing the school newspaper for this month. I've also decided, maybe foolishly, but I think it's worth it, to publish within this class, each class, my own school newspaper so that every person will have an item in it. Even if it's one line with their names at the end. It will be . . . my contribution to the whole school. I think that's worth [doing]. It's worth my extra time . . . because they need those little plugs.

In addition, she made a special effort to honor exceptional individual performance. Ken (described later in this chapter), for example, built a remarkable Viking ship out of wood as his explorers unit social studies project. Kerrie called the project to the attention of the entire class, complimented Ken, and put the ship on display. For several days afterward Ken received the praise of his peers for a job well done. On his part, he exhibited pride in his craftsmanship, a strong intrinsic motivator.

Quality of Activities

Kerrie also became more sensitive to the worthwhileness of activities, choosing ones that made sense to the students educationally. Nothing is more damaging to motivation than to engage in endless busy work. During the study of Colonial America, for example, rather than assigning the students to read textbook descriptions of Colonial life, Kerrie coordinated the reading assignments, which focused on *The Witch of Blackbird Pond*, with social studies activities. To help the students make connections with life during those times, she and the team leader planned a "Colonial Days" festival in the spring. On these two days the students worked in five "stations," engaging in different Colonial crafts, including cooking, tin punching, and candle making. From an instruction and management perspective, what made Colonial Days effective was not only the planned activities, but Kerrie's ability to "overlap." Overlapping is the ability to monitor more than one activity at a time (Kounin, 1970). At the beginning of the period the classes were very excited, and to settle them down Kerrie made a threat, "Class, we don't have to do this; we can just start the next unit and skip this week." Quickly the students settled down and moved into their groups to begin rotating through the activities, which they very much enjoyed doing. As Kerrie demonstrated candle dipping, she kept a close watch on the other groups. Once through with the demonstration she quickly moved to assist the tin punching group; in between visiting the two groups she met with individual students to get them to where they needed to be. Throughout the afternoon, as she moved from one group to the next, complimenting and assisting, she scanned the other groups to make certain the students were engaged or to help where there were problems. It was an exhausting day; it is easy to understand why many teachers avoid enlivening their classes in this manner. Nevertheless, Kerrie was very pleased with how the festival went; at year's end she recalled Colonial Days as the year's best set of activities because of how excited and engaged the students were. It is important to note that had she not been able to handle multiple activities at the same time, it might very well have been one of the year's worst events.

Variety of Methods

Motivation and increased student learning also result from teachers varying their instructional methods (Good & Brophy, 1987). Kerrie liked change. She worked very hard, even before she had solid control of her classes, to vary her instructional methods:

> I think it was in our [university class together] that we talked about all the different methods of learning. So, I'm trying to use all of those: writing, listening, reading. All the different ways you can approach something. [For example,] to bring our unit together the kids are going to do puppet shows, plays, and interviews with Columbus and Magellan. That type of thing. They don't want to do the same thing every day. Neither do I. I can't lecture to them every day. I don't want to, they would die if I did.

When repetition was necessary, she varied her methods as well:

> In most of the things we're doing [right now] it is repetition. I lecture about it; we saw a film about it; we're writing a report about it; we'll do a skit about it. It makes you feel good to have the students doing different things. To see that they're happy or maybe barely excited about doing something different.

Interesting Activities

Activities that are inherently interesting are motivating. As noted in Chapter 3, Kerrie worked very hard to identify appropriate activities, initially for the purpose of improving classroom control. This effort also had a profound impact on student motivation. As mentioned earlier, she began the year planning under the assumption that a good curriculum, one that the students found engaging, would resolve any potential control problems. While this proved to be an illusion, with the result that for a time she became less willing to take instructional risks, the assumption endured in a modified form. She still sought fun and interesting activities, but within the parameters that she felt would allow her to maintain an acceptable level of classroom control.

Basically, three criteria, which operated intuitively until she was questioned about them, informed Kerrie's quest for activities that were motivating. An activity, she said, "has to be interesting. It has to be something I think is fun—fun is always an element in my book. I don't care what. [And, it must be] fairly easy [for them] to understand. Understandable. And that I can teach it."

Positive Teacher Model

Kerrie thought learning should be fun. She modeled a person who enjoyed learning, and she expected the students to share in her pleasure. Nonverbally, she sent the message to students that she liked teaching, enjoyed and respected them, and expected good performance. School was a good place to be. Enthusiasm is a word that easily comes to mind to describe Kerrie's classroom presence. Typically, she was animated— richly alive—when interacting with the students. Without question, she loved teaching. That she respected students was a message sent in various ways: When helping them at their desks, she invariably stooped down so that she could have direct eye contact; she rarely talked down to her students. She physically engaged them, offering a gentle touch on the hand or tap on the shoulder as a sign of reassurance, as if saying, "you can do this, I'm here to help."

DEALING WITH INDIVIDUAL DIFFERENCES

It's frustrating. How long are you supposed to wait? If I waited until everyone finished the assignment, I'd still be waiting. It's [only] the third week of school and there are stragglers. I don't know the cure, either. It's hard when they're so different.

And, four weeks later:

Sometimes when they come up [to my desk] and say, "What can I do next?" I don't know. Go sit down, read a book. That's always a problem, stragglers. As soon as you start something, someone is done and they've done a good job! You can't make them do it over again!

Homogeneous grouping was supposed to make teaching easier for Kerrie; it did not, although at the beginning of the year, before she was fully sensitive to the range of ability in her classes, she thought it did. Assuming that the students within each group (average and low ability) were generally alike in their ability, the strategy she settled on was to keep both groups moving through an identical curriculum at the same pace, but to require more work, in greater depth, and presumably of higher quality of the more able group than of the less able group. Rather quickly, however, she discovered that each class had its own high, middle, and low groups that blended together; each contained a wide range of student ability (as evidenced by the reading scores noted in Chapter 1) and in some fashion she would have to respond to it instructionally. Moreover, differences in ability were compounded by differences in personality and in the value placed on schooling. Kerrie was troubled, for example, when one student would do much of her work in the "last five minutes of class" and at a level far below her ability. This student was quite happy with B grades: "I don't know what to do with her; she needs to be kicked in the butt!"

Initially, the problem of student differences, once Kerrie became aware of it, was simply too overwhelming to deal with at an instructional level; differences seemed to multiply the longer she taught and the better she got to know the students, and so she plowed ahead trying to maintain class order and keep the classes and students in stride: "I'll say to the [more able] kids, you . . . have to wait for the rest of [the class] to get done." In effect, the less able students in each class, or those prone to wasting time, had an inordinate degree of influence over the pace and amount of work accomplished within a given lesson, while those who completed their work were then free to engage in disruptive activity.

When she had to deal with differences, Kerrie relied on ad hoc approaches, only to find exceptions proliferating beyond a manageable level. In effect, while trying to establish a reasonable level of expectation (which is part of adjusting from being a college student to being a junior high school teacher), Kerrie had gone too far, too low, with unhappy results. Personally, she was very frustrated with the situation and perplexed about what to do. As she analyzed the situation, she realized she needed to find a middle ground, which necessitated speeding up the classes, requiring more work, and nudging her standards a bit higher, and then sticking more firmly to them: "I'm learning I need to be stricter in expressing my expectations and sticking to them." And later, "Things are different now . . . it came to me that the more work I give them the better they are. So, I've been loading them down like crazy. I'm trying to require more."

While exceptions continued to be made, they became fewer and were based on greater knowledge of and sensitivity to student potential: "There isn't a written standard, it's the feel I get from the kids. It takes time [to understand what they can do]. Some of them I'm still zoning in on . . . zeroing in on them." For example, with one child she remarked, "You're better than this, I expect better. I gave you an A, but no more; this is really B work, at best. Go sit down and start [doing] A work." With yet another student she took a very different tack: "He's thinking three times as hard [as the brighter kids]. At least he's trying to figure out what words to copy off of the page. He's working harder than the 'smart' kids. So, why not say, 'OK, [even though you didn't do all of the work,] you did great'?"

Throughout Kerrie's first year of teaching, the problem of dealing with individual differences among students continued to be perplexing. It is a problem that never disappears, and perhaps the best that can be expected is that it become manageable. It simply is not possible, given the conditions under which American teachers work, for any teacher, even an expert one, to respond appropriately and well to all students, even when there is an individualized curriculum in place that is reasonably sensitive to differences in ability. There are always other differences that come into play. This view was very difficult for Kerrie to accept. She badly wanted to connect with each child and was very reluctant to give up on any one of them, which is as it should be. By year's end, however, she began to come to terms with the reality that she could not run a program that would meet every child's individual needs. A particularly painful moment came when she realized that at times she would have to choose between trying to meet the needs of one child and those of the rest of her class. In one instance, for example, she finally gave up on a boy who had reasonably good intellectual skills but, after months of concerted teacher effort, had made little if any progress toward gaining self-control: "He's not gotten any better," she sadly concluded. As though conducting triage, she was no longer able to justify continuing to spend an exceptional amount of time with this child, time that would have to be taken away from others who would be more responsive. Nor could she any longer tolerate the disruption of her classes by him; she had him expelled from class: "I'm really sick and tired of him and so is the class. There is a difference [in the classes] when he's not there. So, I figured there is a benefit for 35 other people [to have him gone]."

Jumping ahead, in Kerrie's second year she continued to try to respond to individual differences by keeping the classes moving along together and by making some adjustments in expectations. In addition, she made the problem more manageable by providing a number of legitimate educational options for students who finished their work early to engage in, and by refining her steering group to better control the pacing and direction of lessons. In the second year she had steering groups composed of two groups of two or three students who reflected high-low ability and high-average ability. These students were selected intentionally (in an interview during the late fall Kerrie actually named the students who belonged to the steering groups) based on ability and on the ease with which they could be "read." Based on their actions, Kerrie could tell how well or how poorly a lesson was going, whether to speed it up or slow it down, or whether a change in direction was necessary. In this way she appeared to engage a larger number of students than during the first year, with the result that fewer exceptions were necessary.

ASSESSING STUDENTS' WORK

"I want to be fair, that's what scares me. So much hangs in the balance for the kids." When assessing students' work, teachers make decisions that reflect one or another set of priorities.

- Should effort be most rewarded, or achievement?
- Will grades be norm- or criterion-referenced?
- Are attitudes important?
- Should attention be given to the effects an assessment will have on student motivation and self-esteem?

Sometimes schools will have established policies that serve as guidelines for coming to grips with these issues. For example, some schools rank students, fully expecting to sort according to ability. Rocky Mountain Junior High School, however, had no clear policies whatsoever. Kerrie stepped into a vacuum and could, apparently, do as she pleased; she would have to resolve the conflicting assumptions inherent in grading on her own.

Sorting

Kerrie wanted warm, caring, "fun" relationships to characterize her classes; she was a nurturer who wanted her students to feel good about themselves. Given these values, grading proved to be a troubling, but inevitable, part of teaching. Given that she was not willing to grade students according to ability or achievement — even though they had been homogeneously grouped for placement in her classes — the pivotal problems for Kerrie related to questions of fairness. Those questions in turn were closely related to the problem of accurately determining student ability or potential in relation to student effort. An additional problem centered on the necessity of creating a manageable evaluation system.

Before considering these problems, a word should be said about Kerrie's rejection of sorting as a legitimate assessment aim. Since she had one group of average and one group of low-ability students, a commitment to sorting would necessarily have meant that virtually none of her students would have been deemed worthy of A grades. What she liked about homogeneous grouping was that, at least in principle, "it allows someone [who is] dumb to be smart. It allows them to be the smartest in the class. That's good for some." It did not bother her in the least that she was giving A grades to students who in other classes would be regarded as marginal at best. Nor did it bother her that she gave an unusually large number of A grades to her students. Indeed, it pleased her: After "talking to other teachers and finding out they had given . . . lots of low grades, I was really pleased with the number of As I gave. I was happy with how it came out." It pleased her, in particular, that the grades she gave made the students feel good about themselves; her grades were intended to motivate performance: "They like it. They come up and they are terrified . . . pure terror . . . [and then they] find out they're . . . getting a C instead of an F."

Fairness

However, she did not want to give good grades away; she wanted them to mean something: that the student had performed at a level commensurate with his or her ability. "This kid who sits here — that I have redo his spelling — I could give him an F and he could go off and do his next bad job. Or, I can work with him and he'll get an A and he has his self-esteem. He will learn five new spelling words today." Students who, in her view, did their best deserved an A grade, despite the lower quality of their work compared with other students. But how does one determine whether or not a student is working to potential? And how does one avoid bias in making the judgment? And how does one justify the judgment to students whose work clearly reflects higher quality? These were haunting questions, frequently present at marking sessions.

October: *Fairness is what?* I don't know. (pause) It's grading the kids equally who can be graded against each other. I don't mean "against" but together on the same criteria. It's setting up the criteria and sticking to that. *So, you have this . . . pool of [students] who are held pretty much to the same criteria? How do you decide who is in what group?* I don't know. That's part of the scariness [about grading]. It is [scary]. It's horrible! *How do you know . . . they have this potential?* Very superficial things . . . I have to be honest.

Fairness, for Kerrie, had to do with determining which students had similar ability and then holding them to the same standard of performance. In practice this conception of fairness proved to be extraordinarily complex for Kerrie to implement, not the least of her difficulties being her limited knowledge of the students. For example, when she graded a set of papers requiring judgment about the quality of student work, the act of marking each paper actually necessitated making complex calculations of whether or not the paper reflected good performance for the student and then of whether or not this performance was better, or worse, than that of any other student of roughly similar ability. A partial solution to this problem was that Kerrie minimized the number of papers requiring decisions of this kind and instead emphasized assignments that were judged only on whether or not they were completed, a loose measure of student effort: "Someone will hand in something and I will just check it over to see that it's done, rather than make sure everything is correct [on it]." In addition, she reduced the number of quality judgments to be made by emphasizing tasks for which there were correct answers. Assignments of this kind, particularly worksheets, were seldom demanding for the students. Kerrie's view was that any student who put in the time and effort would obtain the correct answers and therefore would deserve an A grade. Her tests also tended to emphasize correct answers, but they too were written in the belief that the student who put in the effort to learn the material would do well. Sorting was not the intention. In effect, then, this aspect of the issue of fairness came fully into play only in a relatively narrow range of the curriculum, that is, in those few assignments where an assessment of quality had to be made, and at the end of the grading period. At that time, Kerrie frequently thought about the impact of the grade on student motivation and self-esteem and accordingly made adjustments. While Kerrie's approach to grading skirted, to some degree, certain of the problems of fairness, it proved ultimately to be unsatisfactory. She concluded, at year's end, that the approach was "not . . . very good instructionally" and vowed to do more grading, more discriminating between good- and poor-quality work, during her second year of teaching, which she did.

> That's what scares me . . . I know when you see one person's name you most likely identify a grade [with the name]. I try not to [play favorites even though I have them]—I don't like S.'s personality . . . I do like J.'s, isn't it unfair? . . . you want to be easier on someone you like. Or harder on someone you don't.

A second aspect of fairness has to do with avoiding bias when making judgments. Kerrie had her favorites, as all teachers do; and like other teachers she tried to keep her biases in check. Unfortunately, she felt unable to utilize the preferred way to do this: "read everything blind so that you know what the quality is, and then reread it." She simply did not have time to do this (although she made the time to review student work that had been redone): "It's kind of unrealistic, most of the time." Besides consciously striving to set her biases aside, the heavy emphasis on assignments that did not involve quality judgments helped reduce the problem, but did not remove it. The issue, and the internal dialogue that bore it, persisted throughout the year.

> The kids do this all the time. They get a paper back and they look . . . "What did you get?" [They'll notice they did the same quality of work and so] they'll come up and say, "We got different grades." I'll say, "Okay, then I'll change them." Probably [I'll give them] the higher grade . . . it would be unfair not to. I think about [fairness] all the time as I am doing this. Sometimes I'll say, "He did a better job, for him. You could have done it better."
> Sometimes I just feel like I should sit down and write out all my reasons why [a particular paper] should be a certain grade. Then, I should read those and study them.

Justifying what, on the surface, may have appeared to be capricious decisions to the students was, at times, uncomfortable. To some students, Kerrie may have seemed to be a soft touch, easy to persuade to change a grade upward. To others she may have seemed hard and unreasonable. Following the first grading period, Kerrie realized that she needed to be more consistent when making judgments of quality, in part because she inadvertently was communicating the message that quality was relatively unimportant. The transition to higher standards came when she began to be more clear about precisely what she expected and began handing work back that did not meet the standard, insisting that it be redone: "I'm handing [assignments] back and saying, 'If you want an A, this is a C, or this is a B. If you want better [redo it, if not] I'll keep it. I want them to give me better work." In this way, the burden was placed entirely on the student, who, in effect, choose which standard of performance to meet; thereby, Kerrie avoided the necessity of justifying her judgments. Apparently, this approach was effective, although it increased her work load. The students interviewed during the spring uniformly thought of her as a fair teacher. As one student remarked, she is fair "because if you earn an F you get an F. If you deserve an A, you get an A."

Grading System

The system for grading student work that Kerrie developed was a variation of the pattern used during her student teaching. She gave everything a letter grade, not points, thinking that grades, unlike points, tell students precisely how they are doing: "I don't record any number grades, [only] letter grades: A, A−, even A+. Then−I have a calculator−[all I need to do is] push [the grades and] it computes them." She gave a large number of assignments, so the roll book was literally filled each quarter with marks. For the first grading period, each assignment was weighted equally, which quickly became a problem. Obviously some activities were "worth" more than others; some assignments, she said, were "goofy," not worth much at all. In response to the problem Kerrie began making her weightings clear and public, and, in addition, reconsidered marks initially given: "I'm going to go back and put in a different total [for some assignments]. I'm doing them in retrospect." The standards she used to do her retrospective weighting, which were used throughout the other three grading periods, were "time spent" doing the assignment and the "importance" of the assignment.

Based on her experience of having had to "make adjustments as I go" during the first grading period, the second grading period went much more smoothly. She weighted assignments up front and publicly, and clarified her standards and expectations. She still had problems, however: "Sometimes I have a standard in my head that no one could meet." An additional improvement came in the spring when she began working to link her tests more closely to the curriculum, which helped her to more accurately assess student progress as well as to identify topics in which her teaching may have been significantly less effective than she had hoped: "I don't expect them to have to take the grade they have gotten when I don't feel happy with how I presented [the material]." An essential part of this effort involved writing test questions as she taught rather than at the conclusion of a unit, relying on her memory of what she thought had been taught: "That is how I write tests . . . as I go."

Through these changes, Kerrie eventually created a system she found to be generally workable and reasonable, one with which she was more or less well pleased. "I have a good system," she said. But problems of fairness continued to perplex her: "Grading is still kind of a problem with me. I wouldn't mind taking a class on grading. I think grading could be hit much better in college. I'd give that low marks. I just didn't really know what to do, kind of." During her second year, she refined the system and developed a strategy to better meet the challenge of fairness. On assignments where judgments of quality were necessary, Kerrie began writing down in advance precisely what she would look for, and would then attach a point value to the criteria. That value would, for recording purposes, be translated into a letter grade. These criteria and point values would then be written on a small sheet of paper, which was duplicated by a student aide. While reading the assignments Kerrie would write her assessment on these sheets of paper, which would later be given to the students when the graded assignments were returned. For example, if an assignment was worth 50 points (which would be translated into percentages and then grades), on the left-hand side of the paper given to the students would be such items as "neatness" followed by a blank space, a slash, and a point value, something like this "____/5." In the blank Kerrie would write what points the student received of the 5 possible for neatness (5 points equal 10 percentage points or one letter grade). By giving the students the sheets, she let them know precisely what she was evaluating and what she expected: "When a student says, 'Why did I get this [mark]?' I say, 'Where is your paper?'" An additional benefit of this approach was that by explicitly stating the criteria, Kerrie became more consistent in her assessments, which, she said, made grading "much easier for me and fairer to the kids." Consistency was further improved by making comparisons between papers already graded and papers about which she was uncertain.

RELATIONSHIPS WITH PARENTS

[Having parents come into class] is kind of threatening. Don't you think? . . . Probably [I feel this way] because it is my first year and I don't feel that steady about [teaching] anyway. That is honestly how I have felt . . . Yuck! Stay away!

Parents can be threatening to beginning teachers. Despite Kerrie's statement, however, parents seemed to be more surprising and disappointing than threatening to her. Her first parent/teacher conference was most instructive:

I had one stepfather come in with a mother and say, "My wife has been much too easy on this kid. Now, I'm just [going to work] the hell out of him." The poor little kid. He's certainly a good kid, but he is not really [very bright]. My heart goes out to [these children].

Only a few parents attended, which was disappointing: "I don't understand it. I work. Yesterday I had the day off and I was over at my kids' school. I go in, stick my head in the door and see what my child is doing and . . . what the teacher is doing. I do that a lot." Perhaps, she thought, the parents were too intimidated to attend: "I think it just intimidates many parents."

While she did not find parent/teacher conferences particularly threatening, it was difficult to muster up the courage to tell some parents that their children were doing poorly. She was well prepared, however, which made the evening go reasonably well: "I had taken a supply of handouts. So, . . . your child failed this, here it is. I had [examples of work to show, as well]. I had my statistics there in front of me. The most [the parents] could do was to get on me about curriculum . . . [besides, the meetings only lasted] five minutes."

Kerrie began teaching assuming that other parents shared her high level of commitment to and involvement in the education of children. What she found was that the majority of the parents of her students, while well intentioned, were of little noticeable help in their children's schooling. In this, she echoed a common complaint of beginning teachers (Veenman, 1984).

A brief consideration of the family situations of the four students interviewed for this study should help to explain this. Surprisingly, each student lived with both parents. But, not surprisingly, all of the mothers worked outside of the home.

- The father of *Ken*, an outgoing charmer who loved to talk and to help his father on various building projects around the house, worked intermittently as a carpenter and was away frequently for extended periods of time. His mother was, as he put it, "the nurse who hands the tools to the doctor." Apparently, she was a receptionist and practical nurse.
- *Helen*, a quiet, plodding, student who rushed home at the end of the school day to watch her favorite "soap," had no idea what her

father did at a large defense plant, but her mother worked as a custodian in a local church to help support their 10 children.

- *Jerry*, a loner, always on the edges of student activity and acutely aware of living in a very small, run-down house, said that his father worked in some capacity with computers for the state government, while his mother was a receptionist for a used-car dealer.
- *Sally* (the steering group member), a shy, slightly awkward and very sensitive person who was in many respects a model student, said her father worked for a credit union. Her mother was a beautician.

Each of these parents was interested in his or her child's school performance, but none of them was able to be intimately involved in it. According to Kerrie, they simply did not have the time, confidence, or energy to do so. Sally, in particular, was very upset at being a latch-key child and badly wanted to come home and find her mother there more often. In contrast, Ken claimed to like being on his own to watch television, make models, or do whatever he wanted. In general, Kerrie's involvement with parents was infrequent, usually limited to brief encounters at parent/teacher conferences, slightly threatening at worst, and disappointing.

There were two exceptions to this generalization. Happily, a few parents did make extra efforts to be involved in their children's learning and from time to time contacted Kerrie to make certain the children were performing adequately. And, too, there were a few parents who were forced to become involved because of serious problems, usually behavior problems. Kerrie got to know Sean's father, for example, quite well, as did all of Sean's other teachers, the counselors, and the vice principals. Because of Sean's total inability to keep on task — he was supposed to be on medication to calm him down — and his disregard of other students, his father (a businessman and single parent) was frequently contacted for assistance by Kerrie and by other representatives of the school. Finally, he and his son were called in to the school for a meeting with the principal, the two vice principals, and Kerrie. Seeing the meeting through the father's eyes grieved Kerrie: "[I'm certain he thought,] 'They all are here wailing on me and my kid.' That was really a sickening feeling to me . . . you feel so helpless. Now, granted, he is a shitty parent." Watching Sean was even more painful: "Sean was almost in tears at one point. It was like he felt . . . he didn't have a single friend in there. He wouldn't even look at me." But during the meeting, grief turned into anger when the father "tried to pin" Sean's problems on Kerrie. In response, the others quickly redirected the conversation back onto the son. Kerrie left the meeting appreciative of the strong support she received from her administrators, but was nevertheless upset: "It was pretty scary. It was a sickening feeling to be involved in that."

Kerrie began her first year of teaching a little threatened by her students' parents. Gradually, this feeling gave way to disappointment, which in turn was replaced by understanding and a resolve to put a great deal more effort into getting parents involved in the education of their children. She realized one way in which she could do this was to do a better job of informing parents about how their children were doing — both good and bad — and about activities taking place in the classroom. More will be said of this in Chapter 7, but it should be noted that Kerrie began her second year of teaching by routinely phoning at least two parents each school night. This paid off handsomely in improved relations and, although there is no firm evidence to support it, in improved student behavior and performance.

CONCLUSION

To varying degrees, Kerrie had problems with classroom discipline, motivating students, dealing with individual differences among students, assessing students' work, and relationships with parents. Classroom discipline was unquestionably the most pressing problem, but it cannot be viewed in isolation from the others. To be sure, once Kerrie had her classes more or less under control, she was able to redirect some of her energy elsewhere, for example, to thinking of ways of responding more effectively to individual differences. But all the problems were present at once in a shifting classroom kaleidoscope, although Kerrie may not have recognized them for what they were: obstacles to creating the kind of classroom learning environment she desired. Kerrie's movement out of the survival stage of teaching was tied closely to her growing ability to locate a difficulty and formulate it into a problem susceptible to solution, as well to her growing understanding of and ability to carry out alternative means of solving problems. Obviously, how a problem is understood bears heavily on how it is addressed. For example, had Kerrie understood the problem of student motivation exclusively as a reflection of student laziness or of bad parenting, she likely never would have been able to create the "fun" classroom that she sought. Clearly, being able to recognize accurately the obstacles to instructional success and then to respond appropriately to them is a sign of teaching expertise.

Kerrie made solid progress in each of the five problem areas through gaining a deeper understanding of teaching and developing a variety of related teaching skills. Nevertheless, with the exception of developing relationships with parents, the problems persisted throughout the year, but in weakened form. By year's end she had her classes well under control, although at times she felt it was tenuous at best. Student motivation remained a perplexing problem, but here too she made steady, albeit not wholly satisfactory, progress. Without question, however, over the year the students became more engaged in learning and more excited about school. Dealing with differences in student ability continued to be troubling, although by her second year of teaching Kerrie developed a program that significantly reduced the difficulty. The problems of fairness attached to making assessments of student work also persisted, but despite this nagging difficulty, she succeeded in creating a reasonably simple, generally effective approach to and system for grading. Finally, while Kerrie began the year feeling somewhat uneasy about working with parents, by year's end this was generally not an area of concern at all.

For beginning teachers, the significance of coming to terms with these problems is of great importance: One's career rests on it; the more problems a beginning teacher has, the more likely he or she is to leave teaching (Veenman, 1984). The issue is not, however, merely the presence or absence of these and other problems; after all, expert teachers still face the difficulties of discipline and management, and especially of motivating students. Rather, for the beginning teacher, it is seeing that progress has in fact taken place, that there is hope that the classroom can become a decent place to be for student and teacher alike. Where there is no progress, there is no hope; and without hope, all problems are reduced to one: surviving the year.

QUESTIONS FOR CONSIDERATION

1. Which of the problems confronted by Kerrie concern you most? Why? Analyze Kerrie's actions. What would you do differently and why?
2. Consider your appearance, physical presence, and voice: What attributes will you bring to the classroom that will aid you in gaining

control? Do you have any liabilities? What are they and how will you adjust for them?

3. Do you consider yourself to be an optimistic, enthusiastic person? If not, what will you do to communicate to young people the importance of the content you teach?

4. Think back on your own experience as a student. Do you recall times when you found what was being studied intrinsically motivating? What was it about those times that sparked your desire to learn? Does your experience provide any insights, or offer any generalizations, that might help you as a teacher to successfully deal with the problem of motivating students?

5. Do you agree with the generalization that intrinsic motivation is a rarity in schools? If so, is there any reason to strive to create it? What is wrong with trying to stimulate student performance through rewards and punishments of various kinds?

6. Do you agree with Kerrie's decision to play down sorting in her grading scheme? What values will you emphasize when grading student work? As a student, what do you hope for from your teachers when they assess your work?

7. Do you worry about working with parents? Why? Were your own parents, or are you as a parent, difficult for teachers to work with? What are the schooling responsibilities of parents?

ACTIVITIES

1. Good classroom management is generally invisible to the untrained observer. Make arrangements to spend some time observing an expert teacher teach. Note examples of how he or she goes about preventing misbehavior. Does the teacher demonstrate with-it-ness and overlapping? Is the classroom routinized? What are the routines in effect? What other skills discussed in this chapter does the teacher demonstrate?

2. Discuss with a student how a teacher who is considered to be very fair assesses the student's work. What conception of fairness does the student hold? Are there principles or procedures mentioned by the student that potentially might be of use to you? What are they?

5 Coping and Avoiding Burnout

Tuesday, October 21: Like every day Kerrie awakened at 5:45 to a quiet house. She dragged herself out of bed, exercised, showered, and dressed. At 6:25 she went downstairs, fixed something to eat, read part of the morning newspaper, and began to review the day's activities. Her husband came down, sat with her, and asked what needed to be done during the day. Among other things, she reminded him that their son needed to take his gym clothes to school. At 6:45 she went upstairs, brushed her teeth, and went into her children's rooms to kiss them goodbye and wish them a good day. She then walked out the front door. This was the routine that began most every day.

It was quiet as she unlocked the door and entered her bright red Volkswagon. It was a pleasant, crisp morning but too cold to open the sun roof. On this day, as other days, she anticipated the traffic flow: If it flowed smoothly and she pressed the speed limit just a little, she would arrive at work by 7:20; otherwise the school day would begin about 7:30. During the drive she reviewed the day's activities. Since the students were returning from a four-day holiday following back-to-school night, she anticipated that they would be difficult to settle down. The drive helped get her ready psychologically. She was glad to have first-period consultation, which gave her a little more time to get prepared.

She was correct—the students were excited, difficult to settle down, wild. All around her, students chatted happily about their weekends and showed one another items they had brought from home, as she vainly shushed and urged them to quiet down. Some students wandered in late. It was going to be a long day. Finally, she got them settled down and began the day's lesson, but it was a struggle to keep them on-task.

Throughout the day the struggle continued. She was constantly surrounded by students who needed help or who did not listen carefully enough to her directions. As the day progressed, her frustration grew. By afternoon she was nearly frazzled; the students were winning. Seventh period finally arrived, and the end of the day was within sight: Announcements from the office were supposed to begin the period, but often they came late so the teachers never knew quite when to begin class. Kerrie waited, while the students talked noisily. Finally the announcements began. Once these were over, she gave the students a quiz on a movie they had seen. This quieted them down. However, as they finished the quiz, the noise level began to creep up. As Kerrie struggled to get them to begin an independent seat-work assignment, two students were wrestling, and most were chatting. The team leader, whose class was also noisy, walked by and commented, "It's so noisy in here, I'm going crazy!" Finally, after five minutes of near chaos, Kerrie got them settled down, continuously shushing them and commenting, "It's too noisy!" For about 10 minutes they remained settled, but then the noise level again began to rise and yet another play fight suddenly erupted, this time between two girls. When Kerrie's back was turned, some children threw things around the room, and a boy with a cast and a girl with long blonde hair began running about. When the buzzer sounded, indicating day's end, Kerrie had "had it," rather than hold them after class as she had threatened earlier, she let them go, just to get rid of them.

It was, in Kerrie's words, a day that nearly drove her "crazy." She was angry and frustrated. "Today they were just screwing off! All these little toys they have. Wanting to look at each other's stuff. Combs. Brushes. I should take them and hit them on the head with the stupid things! It drives you nuts." She sounded tired, discouraged.

Kerrie was relieved the day was over. As she got into her car for the drive home, she was glad her piano lesson would be Thursday. She just wanted to be home. The drive was calming and settling, a pleasant break. She arrived home slightly after 4:00 and was greeted by her children. While they did their homework, she corrected papers and marked grades in her roll book. She then finished reading the newspaper and began, with the children's help, to prepare dinner. Her husband arrived home just in time to wash up and sit down to eat. They finished eating about 7:00, leaving two hours before the children's bed time for family activities. At 9:00 the children were in bed, and Kerrie began reading to them as she did nearly every evening. She did "double duty," as she called it, when reading to her children: The books were ones she planned to read to her classes or was thinking about reading to them. A bit before 10:00 she got ready for bed, did her exercises, and stretched out to read for 10 or 15 minutes before falling asleep.

With slight variations—once a week she and her husband went out for the evening, for example—this was the pattern Kerrie followed throughout much of the year. Fortunately, the school day described was exceptional; most classes went much better. Nevertheless, it does reflect the kind of pressures teachers, particularly married female teachers, are under, to varying degrees, day in and day out throughout the school year. Certain parts of the year are more difficult than others: before and after holidays, spring time when good weather arrives after a long winter. Similarly, some days of the week and times of the day are more difficult than others, such as Mondays and Fridays, especially in the afternoon.

Given this situation, John Goodlad (1984) asks an especially appropriate question:

> Is it realistic to expect teachers to teach enthusiastically hour after hour, day after day, sensitively diagnosing and remedying learning difficulties? During each of these hours . . . teachers make 200 or more decisions. During each day of the week, many secondary teachers meet hour after hour with successive classes of as many as 35 students each (Kerrie had 36 in her afternoon classes.) As one teacher said to me recently, "It is the sheer emotional drain of interacting with 173 students each day that wears me down." (p. 194)

Is it realistic to expect this of teachers? A second question is even more to the point for beginning teachers: Will they be able to endure until the end of the year, let alone teach enthusiastically? Clearly, in order to survive the year and keep from becoming overwhelmed, Kerrie, like other beginning teachers, had to cope with a wide range of problems that were new to her. This chapter focuses on Kerrie's coping strategies, and on how she managed to make life within Rocky Mountain Junior High School tolerable, even enjoyable, on most days.

How Kerrie coped needs to be understood in the light of the personal characteristics noted earlier. Kerrie asserted that she had always wanted to be a teacher. She thought of herself as a teacher long before beginning to teach. She brought to her first year of teaching an internalized role identity through which she made sense of the environment and by which she judged the appropriateness of her actions. Along with it came a teacher common sense — this is what teachers do — that was tested for its reasonableness, utility, and accuracy throughout the first year.[1] Kerrie responded to the problems she faced in what were to her commonsensical, "natural" ways, only later to find out through teaching whether her sense was indeed common or exceptional. And so she often reacted intuitively to her environment and the problems she faced, a

---

[1]For a discussion of teacher common sense, see Crow (1987).

tendency encouraged by the work context itself: "When you ask me [why I do certain things] I can come out with [reasons] but I don't think about them." When intuition failed, she began to respond reflectively to her situation in the quest for alternatives.

Kerrie demonstrated seven different types of coping strategies during the survival stage of teaching:

environmental simplification
stroke seeking and withdrawal
context restructuring
compromise and compliance
skill improvement (discussed partially in Chapter 4)
problem disownment
laughter and emotional release.

These were, with the clear exceptions of skill improvement and context restructuring, primarily intuitive responses (reactions to problems) that over time became habitualized when they "worked." The fact that such responses become habitual is of considerable importance to the development of teaching expertise and professionalism (Pollard, 1982). Each will be discussed in turn and in relationship to the problems and work conditions discussed earlier.

ENVIRONMENTAL SIMPLIFICATION

One of the ways in which Kerrie responded to the problems of teaching, particularly the intense work pace and the student and administrator pressure to conform to role expectations and the resultant contradictions with her own values, was to simplify the environment by reducing the number of demands that came into play at any given moment. There were three ways in which she did this, one "natural" or intuitive, and two somewhat reflective. She simplified the environment by:

1. Ignoring problems
2. Selectively responding to them
3. Systematizing or routinizing aspects of the environment

A brief description of each follows.

Unthinkingly, Kerrie ignored some of the pressures placed on her. She turned them off. For instance, it was in this way that she softened the impact of being watched and evaluated constantly, particularly by the principal: "I don't think about it very much. See, this is one of those things I can't do much about . . . so, I don't bother to think about it." Later, she felt confident enough to assert:

> I behave as though he (the principal) doesn't exist, honestly. I wouldn't be doing anything differently if he was standing outside my door. And that is true. I don't even think about it. He can walk through my class any time and I'd be glad to say why we're doing what we're doing. That's not . . . my problem . . . at all.

Generally, problems she felt were beyond her control were accepted as inevitable and set aside: "If I can't solve [a problem] I just . . . live with it. That's my coping mechanism."

At other times, she chose more mindfully to not attend to some work demands. For instance, she selectively responded to student misbehavior: "*Are some kinds of misbehavior OK, and others not?* Yes . . . definitely. I perpetuate [some misbehavior] because it seems like there are so many other things to attend to. [For example,] like sitting . . . reading a book, that's not disturbing anybody." And further:

> I'm really busy right now. I have a lot of papers to correct, tomorrow's mid-term and I have to fill out all these papers and I don't write "pass" or "fail" so I've got to estimate all those grades! (laughter). And so, instead of running around and keeping people quiet and reading, I just let them go because I have to do [so much right now].

Unfortunately, the standard driving this decision was a pragmatic, rather than an educational, one. Another time she was quite upset by the performance of several of her students on a test and by the large number of students who simply did not take it. In response to this situation,

> I didn't even bother to have them make it up. I should have had them do it, I guess. But I didn't care by then. I was too upset. So, I said, "If you do well [on the next test], whatever grade you get, you'll get for both . . . it's like I'm just throwing out the first because it was so bad.

A third way in which Kerrie simplified the environment was by routinizing or systematizing much of it so she would not have to think about how to respond to a particular situation or event every time it came up. Instead, she could simply react automatically. She did this, as noted in Chapters 3 and 4, through an extended and difficult period of trial and error.

STROKE SEEKING AND WITHDRAWAL

Kerrie entered Rocky Mountain Junior High School a loner, a tendency encouraged by the work context and by the teacher role as established within the school. She had not expected to become fast friends with a large group of teachers. She had, however, hoped that she would be given a measure of support and some critical feedback that would help her develop professionally. In this she was mostly disappointed. Initially she saw in the occasional team meetings the possibility of initiating satisfying professional interaction, but meetings were infrequent and agendas set. Moreover, she did not think it "her place" to call team meetings, perhaps fearing offending the team leader, and wanting to fit in:

> I . . . feel we should have [team meetings] just because you end up talking about things you don't normally talk about. And it might bring up things. I don't know what, but suggestions [about teaching]. *So, why don't you have them?* It's not my responsibility to call them. I don't want to be a pest. If I were the team leader I'd have them not every week, but every two weeks, for sure—when I'm the team leader! (laughter).

In response to this situation, Kerrie sought feedback and found support elsewhere: teachers with whom she shared inservice classes, family, and friends. Inservice classes proved to be a boon, in part because others in attendance shared her concerns:

> I get more strokes going to the stupid inservice things, with people I don't even know. *But you talk and share things?* Yes, I would say that I have a couple of people I'm closer to at those [meetings than here]. *And they're from different schools?* Yes, one of them is not even a teacher, he's a counselor.

For emotional support she relied heavily on her mother: "I can always talk to my mom [who is a teacher]. She's always open. She [calls me] all the time . . . when she's really mad at the people she works with or mad at the P.T.A. . . . . or something like that. I [also talk with] . . . my friends, Catherine or Mary." Ultimately, however, Kerrie was on her own; she had to meet her own standards: "There's a personal feeling of knowing [that something has gone well]. You set a standard for yourself and you meet the standard."

In effect, Kerrie compartmentalized her life. In one slot was Rocky Mountain Junior High School, where she was somewhat satisfied with the emotional support and the personal and professional confirmation, albeit infrequent, that came from the students. She gave up the expectation that she would enjoy open, professional relationships with other teachers on the staff. In another slot were her home and family: "I think it's really strange but that's just how it works, it's like a different life." She did not, for example, "talk shop" with her husband unless it was to share an anecdote: "When I do [share with him], it's usually anecdotal type things, about something that has happened in school or even something interesting that we are doing like making filmstrips, something out of the ordinary." And later:

> I never ever talk to my husband about school. He'd probably be startled if he knew the things I do. It's because by the time I get home [the problems I'm dealing with] are gone. It's like they exist out here (at Rocky Mountain Junior High School). I really don't like to talk about them. By the time I get home, I'm home.

The drive home helped her set her problems aside; it was a time of transition from work to home, a time within which to wind down. Home and family served as a break from school, a haven, a place where she could go to be loved and supported unconditionally. Somewhere in between these two slots stood her inservice coursework, which was secure and fun, an escape from Rocky Mountain Junior High, yet connected to her professional development.

CONTEXT RESTRUCTURING

Kerrie could do little about two of the most significant sources of her management and control problems: large class size and the layout of the building. What she could do was try to create physical arrangements within the classroom that reflected the high value she placed on appropriate student interaction and activity that she associated with having a "fun" class. To this end, she experimented with various seating patterns. For example, she clustered the desks, forming in the afternoon class six teams of six students each, with a rotating team captain responsible for passing out and gathering materials and for reminding the team members to keep on-task. Despite initial student resistance, this arrangement encouraged class "unity": "There is not unity in rows. There's a possibility [of achieving it] in tables." Unfortunately, this arrangement also created a set of unanticipated problems, which led after three months to a return to desks in rows. To her surprise, the table arrangement encouraged off-task behavior — the students were unable to monitor themselves effectively. Nevertheless, the cohesiveness and friendliness encouraged by this arrangement endured.

As Kerrie moved through the survival stage of teaching, particularly as her knowledge of the students and available materials increased, it became possible for her to alter the curriculum she had inherited. At the beginning of the year she had no choice but to teach the units given to her, trusting that they were appropriate for her students. Besides, she wanted to fit in with the team. Gradually, she restructured much of the curriculum to better reflect her values and better respond to her students. For example, by mid-year she felt secure enough to take a two-week break from the required English text:

> I'm taking the rest of this week and next week and just stopping book work. When I did my evaluation (student evaluations of her teaching), they said, "Why don't we play more games and do things other than—especially in English—go through the book? That's about all we've done."

At other times, she altered the curriculum by excluding some topics and adding other ones.

COMPROMISE

One striking characteristic of the survival stage of teaching is tension and conflict associated with clashes between personal values and institutionalized role requirements and expectations. Each beginning teacher must negotiate his or her place within the institution; compromise is necessary. But how much compromise? Compromise of what values? And to what purpose?

Recall that the context and the problems she faced pressed Kerrie to be, in her words, "hard as nails." But as she thought about herself she knew this was not a role she could play easily, even while she thought she should play it: "I'm just not a hard-as-nails person. I see people who do that and I think that it's something I need to strive to do but I just don't know if I can do it." She vacillated back and forth, giving her students a mixed message, which only sharpened the difficulties she encountered during the survival stage of teaching: The students wondered, who was this person teaching? Gradually, she came to terms with the dilemma:

> I don't want to dread certain people in school. They are not going to make school a miserable place for me. So, by laying down some rules I feel like I can [maintain a decent environment]. I have to maintain con-

trol of [the class]. So, yes, I'm being tough. But, they still know what I'm like [although] I'm still going to be stricter.

While she could not be "tough as nails," she could become "stricter," which meant setting some rules and tenaciously sticking to them. It was only in this way, ultimately, that she could achieve the fun class that she desired. She gave up something to gain something even more valuable.

A related set of compromises arose as a result of the school's commitment to Assertive Discipline (noted in Chapter 3) and Kerrie's need early in the year for ideas about controlling her classes. Assertive Discipline was one of the approaches to discipline presented and critiqued during Kerrie's teacher education (see Canter, 1977). The approach involves both an attitude — that teachers must be "assertive" in their efforts to maintain classroom order — and a set of procedures, including, as practiced within Rocky Mountain Junior High School, the writing of a student's name on the board at the first infraction, followed by a check next to the name for a second infraction, and after a third warning, a referral to the principal's office for punishment. When Kerrie entered Rocky Mountain Junior High School, she brought with her a strong dislike for Assertive Discipline, which she perceived as contrary to her teaching values; she did not want to be a "police officer." And yet, as the year progressed she realized that policing was part of teaching, an unpleasant part to be sure, but nevertheless inescapable. This realization did not, however, alter her opposition to Assertive Discipline. Rather, the grounds of her complaint changed from its being a mode of policing, to its being a somewhat ineffective mode:

> P., one of the other [team teachers], said, "I dislike Assertive Discipline because it gives them permission to be bad three times." That is my problem. As soon as I write a name on the board, they say, "How many checks do we need by our name?" I think, . . . dammit, that's not the point! It's just pissed me off! So, I think I might as well write [the student's] name, check, check, check! Right? That has really gotten on my nerves.

Her first compromise — accepting the necessity of policing — set the stage for a second compromise. She would use Assertive Discipline techniques, but not in the same form used throughout the school:

> You've noticed I narrowed it down. I . . . say their names a couple of times. But, once their name is on the board they know the next time that's it. The first time . . . I write it up there you move away from wherever you're talking—that's usually the problem.

On some occasions compromise was strictly one-sided; Kerrie simply had to do as she was told. For example, she found the school hall pass policy especially irritating, but complied begrudgingly:

> I understand it but I dislike it. That . . . stupid hall pass business. If I want the kid to go to the bathroom, I want the kid to go to the bathroom! I don't want to write him a note to go to the bathroom, to the library, to get paper, to get a drink!

Two additional examples of compromise deserve mention because of their impact on Kerrie — she felt guilty. The first example arose when she became overwhelmed with the work load and found it necessary to give up what she knew to be a desirable educational practice:

> I expected them to do a report first of all in pencil. Have me check it off. Then, take it, [rework it,] and recopy it in ink. *You read everything twice?* I started reading them all, then I immediately quit. It's too mind boggling. Eight reports times sixty kids twice. If I were to do that twice! . . . eight reports in two weeks! I gave up on that. Finally, I just started checking them off if they were done.

At this moment Kerrie came face to face with the realization that she could not do all that she thought she should, or that was expected of her, which produced guilt feelings.

The second example, noted in Chapter 3, came as a result of inadvertently buckling under to strong and persistent student pressure:

> It always seems like I have an idea of what kind of work I want to get back from kids and they don't seem to understand that that is *exactly* what I'm going to want. Like they don't give me the quality that I'm asking for. Then I say, well, I guess they can't do it and so . . . instead of grading them down, I lower my [standards] for them and give them higher grades than they really should get.

She felt bad about the situation once she recognized it, and resolved to alter it, but changing student expectations proved to be very difficult, particularly since she had waffled during the early part of the year.

SKILL IMPROVEMENT

Obviously, as noted in Chapters 3 and 4, the improvement of a wide range of skills is essential to creating a positive learning environment for both teacher and students. If the novice teacher does not learn how to manage and motivate students and how to design and present appropriate and stimulating lessons, the role and responsibilities of teacher, as institutionalized, will break the beginning teacher. Failure in this area results in arrested development; the beginning teacher may forever be condemned to the purgatory that is the survival stage of teaching. There are other necessary skills, slighted by teacher education programs, where the goal is more than survival. These are skills associated with maintaining and enhancing one's sense of self as a worthwhile and contributing member of a profession. Put negatively, these are skills associated with staying alive professionally and avoiding burnout. Even as a beginning teacher, Kerrie was very much aware of the dangers of burnout. For example, following a meeting with a group of angry, frustrated teachers, Kerrie commented, "I always think to myself, I am smart enough not to get into that big burnout. I really think I am. But then I look at these [other teachers]. Some . . . of these people . . . have thought that too."

Three sets of skills bear mention at this point: One critical set has to do with planning and pacing lessons; a second set, with being able to adjust to changing circumstances; and a third set, with setting reasonable expectations for self and for others.

Planning and Pacing

One key to Kerrie's eventual movement out of the survival stage of teaching was that she became more skilled as a planner, which, as noted in Chapter 3, had a profound effect on how well or how poorly her classes went, and also significantly influenced the quality of her professional life. Obviously, having students perform and behave better makes life much better for teachers. But there is more at issue here. Kerrie began to plan with greater sensitivity to her own emotional, intellectual, and professional needs. She felt much more secure about teaching when she planned well in advance, for instance. Once she got to know her students and content better, this became possible. She began planning for the winter term fully six weeks in advance and was always far enough ahead so that if something came up unexpectedly, it was only a minor disruption: "I plan well enough ahead that it's not urgent if [something doesn't] get done."

There were other changes as well. As mentioned earlier, planning, for Kerrie, was primarily a matter of creating or selecting and sequencing teachable activities. Goals and objectives, when not contained in textbooks or adopted units, were implicit and taken for granted. As the year progressed it became clear that one of her implicit aims was to select or create activities that would not only stimulate student interest but also keep her interested and intellectually alive. Moreover, she mixed activities that demanded a great deal of teacher time and effort with activities that demanded little time and effort. By doing this she could catch up on grading or other unfinished tasks. During one class period, for instance, in which the students were extremely busy, she "graded a bunch of papers, did some policing. . . . It wasn't very hard on me." She also built in psychological breaks. Quiet activities were sprinkled in between noisy activities, and small-group with large-group and seat-work activities. Some class periods were also easier on her: "Different periods are breaks," she said.

She also parceled out her energy, perhaps intuitively, choosing to focus on one or another student at different times, realizing she could not possibly respond to all during any given period. The negative side of this strategy was that she tended to respond most frequently to students with insistent problems and to those who showed good results comparatively quickly:

> What I have done is, I take turns at whom to focus on. *Explain that.* OK. I've given up on M. for now; he's not doing anything. I'm sure there is going to come a time when I'll be ready to work with him again. But I'm not now. He's just wasting my time. I won't have it. *So, S. is your focus now?* Yes. Because there is progress.

Flexibility

The second set of skills has to do with the ability to adjust to changing circumstances. Reflecting their insecurity and uncertainty, novice teachers tend to hold tightly to lesson plans, routines, and institutional rules and regulations. Initially, Kerrie was no different. As noted, at the beginning of the year she held tightly to an inherited curriculum, which at times proved less than satisfactory. Gradually, however, she loosened her grip as she recognized that the students were not responding as she had hoped and that change was necessary. But before adjusting her grip, Kerrie went through a transition period in which she tried to keep the curriculum intact by making innumerable small adjustments in it for individual students. Only in this way could she achieve a measure of success. Her solution, then, was to hold tightly to the curriculum even while privately and quietly making changes in it: adjustments in assignments, expectations, or even activities designed for individual students. This was not, however, a satisfying solution. As noted previously, too many exceptions were being made, albeit justifiable ones, and Kerrie found she could no longer maintain her grip—the program itself had to be changed, and she changed it. By year's end, she seemed to settle into a comfortable position. She had a program laid out in advance of teaching, but "once interactive teaching [began, her plan moved] to the background" (Clark & Peterson, 1986, p. 266). Like expert teachers, she was able to take advantage of serendipitous moments in the classroom; she became more of an "opportunistic planner" (Berliner, 1986, p. 11).

Upon reflection, Kerrie regretted sticking so tightly to the units given to her at the beginning of the year: "I look back on the beginning of the year and think, 'Oh Horrors!'" *Why?* "I was just so unprepared for [the problems I faced] and I took other people's, like [the team leader's] word for how the first unit was going to go. I look back and I think, 'What a waste of three weeks in social studies.'" While she regretted this decision, ultimately there was no other reasonable alternative. She had to begin somewhere, and she had to teach something. What is important is that in the face of a number of student problems, rather than hold even tighter to the curriculum, she recognized weaknesses within it and adjusted it accordingly.

Reasonable Expectations of Self and Others

The third set of skills has to do with the ability to maintain reasonable expectations of self and others. The individual teacher must recognize that there are limits to what any one person can accomplish. There is, of course, a danger here: Expectations can become so low that poor teaching may be justified or poor student performance and behavior excused, or so high that failure and frustration are inevitable. Kerrie expected some lessons to go badly, materials not to be available, and speakers to show up at the wrong times: "If you make mistakes, regroup and press forward," which is precisely what she did. She did not expect to know everything necessary to be an outstanding teacher her first year: "I see other teachers with [excellent teaching] skills but they didn't start off with them. That takes time to learn yourself." In a related vein, she was able to recognize and celebrate her own progress, which was often difficult when so many things did not go as intended: "I'm making progress. [My ability to control the class is] moving along. It's come a long way. It's kind of been moving up steadily the last few months." She also became more reasonable in what she expected of her students. Being a mother, she knew that young people will, from time to time, misbehave; after all, "they're kids. Brats but . . . still kids. You have to remember that they are children so that you understand what they're doing."

PROBLEM DISOWNMENT

At times Kerrie made her environment more tolerable by disowning problems or shifting responsibility for them away from herself, a common teacher response (Kindsvatter, et al., 1988). To a degree this is a reasonable response to a complex situation. At a time when there are ever-increasing demands placed on teachers, it is difficult not to become overwhelmed and to accept blame for all sorts of problems beyond teachers' control.[2] On the other hand, it is also easy to shift too much responsibility or blame onto others. Parents, for example, are often disparaged by teachers for not doing an adequate job with their children. Students, too, are frequently blamed for failures. What is difficult is to establish and maintain a reasonable level of personal responsibility for what transpires within the classroom.

Wisely, after the prolonged struggle with Sean (described in Chapter 4), Kerrie recognized that her responsibilities were limited and referred him to others for help. Following this decision, she remarked with a sigh of relief, "He's not my problem [now]." From time to time, however, Kerrie may have disowned problems prematurely or dodged her responsibility for them. For example, she felt bad that she had her students spend so little time writing. "I don't have my kids write much." She said she neglected writing because she spent "so much time correcting it" and just did not feel able to carry out this responsibility in the face of the others that pressed in upon her. But rather than accept the decision as an unfortunate temporary compromise, she pointed an accusing finger at the students who did not appreciate the work she did correcting their writing: "You know what happens [when I return their papers]? 'Oh, look at that,' crumple, crumple and in the garbage [it goes after they've seen the grade]." So, why bother, she thought. Similarly, when Kerrie angrily commented on the laziness of her students, she appeared to be shifting blame. Another time, after a large number of students received failing grades on an assignment, Kerrie irritably placed blame on the team leader who presented the unit plan to her, "This whole system was not my idea."

LAUGHTER AND EMOTIONAL RELEASE

While Kerrie had "desperate moments" that made her question the wisdom of teaching in a junior high school — "Sometimes I think I will not really be happy until I'm teaching high school" — for the most part

---

[2]The shifting of responsibilities onto the schools is discussed in Bullough (1988), Chapter 1.

she maintained throughout the year her ability to laugh at herself and with the students. "I let them do stupid things and then laugh, and then it's over. Instead of getting mad [at them]. [Either way] the incident is still over and probably wouldn't happen again. So, what is the point in getting furious over it?"

For all teachers, but especially beginning teachers, there is simply no substitute for humor. On Kerrie's birthday a group of students arranged with the custodian to gain admission into her classroom early in the morning. When she opened the door to begin the day she found her room in total disarray: "They came and 'tee-peed' my room. They moved all the desks into the center and wrapped tape all around them. All the tape I had was wrapped all around them!" Rather than be angry, however, she was delighted: "I called [the perpetrators] out of class and had them come down and [another teacher] took a picture of them standing out in the middle of it all. I left it here all day. I made them sit on the floor. It was really fun. It was really a fun day." Kerrie expected teaching to be fun and worked hard to make it so. "First we read the magazine that you saw. We all sat on the floor and I assigned them parts. It's fun. They loved it. It's fun, it's fun." Upon reviewing the transcripts of the interviews with Kerrie, perhaps the most distinguishing characteristic is the large amount of laughter. Laughter was common in the classroom as well.

In addition, Kerrie occasionally expressed her anger and frustration in class. For example, during one observation she seemed particularly angry and short with the students. When questioned about her behavior, she remarked, "Yesterday things were kind of noisy. So, I wanted to have a little less noise today. Some of them have just got such shitty attitudes. It just really makes me mad! Like J. P. So, [my frustration] kind of builds up and I get mad [at the students]. Then, it kind of releases. Kind of comes and goes." Such times, however, were very rare and only followed an extended period during which frustrations would simmer until they boiled over.

CONCLUSION

The coping strategies Kerrie developed played an essential part in helping her survive the school year. They served her well as she attempted to balance her own needs and interests with those of her students and the school. There were occasions, however, when despite her coping ability, she was nearly awash by the problems and work requirements that pressed upon her — problems and demands that are part of living and working within a large and complex bureaucracy that produce days like the one following back-to-school night. Fortunately, however, these occurrences became progressively less frequent, especially after the Christmas break, indicating movement out of the survival stage of teaching.

Kerrie not only survived the year, but in many respects she thrived, which is remarkable given the challenges of the first year of teaching and the limited amount of help she received in meeting them. Clearly, she liked what she was doing, despite those aspects of the job that were troubling: "I talk to someone about teaching and pretty soon I'm just like this, I'm smiling and laughing and I tell them how *wonderful* it is, then how much fun it is, you can't do anything but love it! It's work, but *my kind*, I guess." Indeed, the year went so well that her negative attitude toward teaching in a junior high school turned around dramatically. She was amazed, when questioned in the spring, by her change in attitude:

> Have I turned around! I said [I wanted to leave the junior high school] under survival conditions. I'm not there anymore. You can do things here you cannot do [in a high school]. *So, that was escape talk?* Yes, it was—"I can't handle this, this is not my element!" Now, I feel like I can. I'm on top of it. I'm going to do much better. Isn't it exciting! I think, why did I think that [high school] was such a utopia?

While Kerrie felt very good about her progress, some fears still hovered in the distance. One was burnout. There are better and worse ways of surviving the first year. Some ways lead to dying professionally. Kerrie wondered, for example, if after a few years she would become like some of the other teachers she observed, who hid behind their desks and were disengaged from the students and from teaching.

Teacher burnout has been a topic of considerable interest over the past decade (see Farber, 1984). Unfortunately, it defines a serious problem inaccurately, perhaps perniciously. The image is one of each teacher being a candle that gradually burns down, flickers, and dies in isolation, as though burning out is a natural conclusion to a teaching career. Thus, the problem of burnout is tied to a loss of individual energy, commitment, and strength: It signals a loss of the ability to cope—the teacher simply gives up trying to manage the job. Understood in this way, the solutions to burnout are tied to individual teachers learning how to manage stress and perhaps to therapy. Attention is shifted away from the conditions of work that produce burnout—isolation, rapid work pace, and so on—and the realization that these conditions can best be improved through teachers working together for change becomes illusory. To be sure, the development of coping strategies is important, but the ability to cope as an individual is a poor substitute for teacher collegiality, for teachers working closely with and helping one another.

Kerrie's concern about burnout was legitimate, especially when viewed in the light of her admission that she really did not know how she coped, she just did it: "I don't know what I do that helps me cope. I don't know. . . . " *You just do it?* "Yes." Clearly, the contexts within which teachers work either enhance or constrain opportunities to develop professionally. While Kerrie was well on her way by year's end to becoming expert in a variety of teaching skills—planning, classroom management, and so on—she accomplished this almost despite the structure within which she worked. Considering that she was generally left on her own, it is easy to imagine that had she been a different kind of person—less dedicated, energetic, determined, confident, or intelligent—her trial and error, experimental approaches to problem solving and her necessary reliance on intuition might have resulted in the development of as many bad instructional habits as good ones; for instance, compromises that would have resulted in the acceptance of poor quality work and that would ultimately lead to personal and professional failure. Near year's end Kerrie recognized that some aspects of her work context would need to be changed if she was to remain professionally vital. "Sometimes," she said, "the answer is not changing yourself. The answer is changing the environment." But then, she quickly added, "some things you can't change."

QUESTIONS FOR CONSIDERATION

1. Compare your days to Kerrie's. Is your life more or less hectic? Is your home a place where you can go for support and strength? Do you have individuals with whom you can talk over your feelings? What kind of support can you expect on the job?
2. How do you cope with trying situations? Do you use strategies similar to Kerrie's or do you have some different ones? If so, what are they? Does one strategy or cluster of strategies dominate?
3. How are the strategies you use likely to influence your personal and professional development?

ACTIVITIES

1. Think of a time during your life or a situation when you were under a great deal of pressure but performed tolerably, if not admirably, well. Make a list of what factors helped make the situation turn out

well. Star those factors that depended on the cooperation of others. Check those factors that were wholly reflections of your resources alone. Are there more stars or checks? Would a similar pattern be desirable during your first year of teaching? Why or why not?

2. Interview a beginning teacher and an experienced teacher. Ask each to describe the teaching problem or situation they find most troubling, why it is troubling, and how they deal with it. Assess their responses in the light of the implications of their actions for their own personal and professional development, and for student learning and development.

6 Becoming Professional

The image we see emerging from research and theory is that of the teacher as professional. We use this term to refer to practitioners who specialize in designing practical courses of action to serve the needs of a particular client group, and whose success depends on their ability to manage complexity and solve practical problems. (Clark & Yinger, 1987, p. 360)

Arguments for the professionalization of teaching are enjoying a prominent place in current discussions of educational reform. From the Holmes Group to the Task Force on Teaching as a Profession, of the Carnegie Forum on Education and the Economy, the message is the same: If Americans want schools that are genuinely educative, then teaching must become a profession (Holmes Group, 1986). The Task Force on Teaching as a Profession, in its publication, *A Nation Prepared: Teachers for the 21st Century* (1986), noting the relationship between autonomy and accountability, put it this way: Americans must "restructure schools to provide a professional environment for teaching, freeing them to decide how best to meet state and local goals for children while holding them accountable for student progress" (p. 3). This chapter focuses on the teacher role presented to Kerrie when she entered Rocky Mountain Junior High School, particularly the professional meaning of that role and how she came to terms with it. Several events that took place during the year that let Kerrie know what her proper place was within the institution will be described. First, however, we will explore professionalism as background for the discussion of Kerrie's experience.

TEACHER PROFESSIONALISM

The characteristics of a profession can be stated quite succinctly (Task Force on Teaching as a Profession, 1986):

Professional work is characterized by the assumption that the job of the professional is to bring special expertise and judgment to bear on the work at hand. Because their expertise and judgment is respected and they alone are presumed to have it, professionals enjoy a high degree of autonomy in carrying out their work. They define the standards used to evaluate the quality of work done, they decide what standards are used to judge the qualifications of professionals in their field, and they have a major voice in deciding what program of preparation is appropriate for professionals in their field. . . . [Moreover,] because professionals themselves are expected to have the expertise they need to do their work, organizations that employ professionals are not typically based on the authority of supervisors, but rather on collegial relationships among the professionals. This does not mean no one is in charge, but it does mean that people practicing their profession decide what is to be done and how it is to be done within the constraints imposed by the larger goals of the organization. (pp. 36, 39)

In short, then, professionals possess expertise and judgment. Because of these attributes, they enjoy a high degree of autonomy, which includes the responsibility for establishing the standards by which the quality of practice is determined. And finally, collegiality, rather than supervisor control, characterizes the community of professionals.

An additional word should be said about autonomy. The case for autonomy is not simply that professionals deserve autonomy because of possessing expertise or judgment, as the Task Force on Teaching as a Profession argues, although these qualities are important. Rather, autonomy is a necessary condition for effective performance, given the indeterminancy of the knowledge professionals possess: It is not neatly reducible to technique or to rules governing appropriate behavior. Inevitably, without autonomy the quality of performance suffers.

It is not simply because professions lay claim to a body of knowledge that they must exercise self-control. Boreham explains that it is the *indetermination* of that knowledge—its inability to be reduced to rules or prescriptions for practice—that is the most powerful basis for professions' arguments that they must have autonomy from administrative control in determining occupational tasks and functions. (Darling-Hammond, 1985, p. 212)

The case for professionalism as a central component of educational reform is based on the belief that anything short of the creation of a large, committed group of professional teachers will not be equal to the challenges presently facing America and American education. Again, referring to *A Nation Prepared* (Task Force on Teaching as a Profession, 1986):

If our standard of living is to be maintained, if the growth of a permanent underclass is to be averted, if democracy is to function effectively
into the next century, our schools must graduate the vast majority of
their students with achievement levels long thought possible for only the
privileged few. The American mass education system, designed in the
early part of the century for a mass-production economy, will not succeed unless it not only raises but redefines the essential standards of
excellence and strives to make quality and equality of opportunity com-
patible with each other. (p. 3)

To meet this challenge, Americans must recognize

two essential truths: first, that success depends on achieving far more
demanding educational standards than we have ever attempted to reach
before, and second, that the key to success lies in creating a profession
equal to the task—a profession of well-educated teachers prepared to
assume new powers and responsibilities to redesign schools for the future. Without a profession possessed of high skills, capabilities, and
aspirations, any reforms will be short lived. (p. 2)

These are heady words. Without question, to realize the aim of
creating a teaching profession, schools and the conditions under which
teachers work will need to be changed. Some of the changes necessary
will be hinted at in the section that follows. At this juncture, however, it
is important to underscore a point made earlier: There are better and
worse ways of surviving the first year of teaching. Better ways lead to
the development of professional values and ideals; worse ways lead toward isolation and withdrawal into the security of the classroom.

Developing a genuine teaching profession, something that reflects
more than just a rhetorical flourish, requires work on two fronts simultaneously: The first is that teachers' self-understanding and the ideals
that inspire action must come to reflect the values of a developing professionalism; and the second is that the conditions of work must be
changed so that they enhance rather than inhibit professionalism. Neither
front can be ignored without dire consequences. Ultimately, Kerrie's
effort—like that of all beginning teachers—to come to terms with the
question of what kind of teacher she would be was answered in ways
that reverberated outward, affecting other teachers; her actions necessarily either enhanced or impeded teacher professionalism. The message
we receive from Kerrie is that while her work conditions did not generally foster professionalism, nonetheless she aspired to develop and live
by a set of professional ideals.

BEING TREATED LIKE
AND ACTING LIKE A TEACHER

Much has been written about the influence of the "hidden curriculum" of schooling on students (Apple, 1979). Students, we are told, are taught to embrace a set of values built into the structure of schooling itself: They are incidental or concomitant learnings; the medium of schooling is the message. Students are taught to be passive and unengaged in learning by the way in which school life is organized through bells, lines, rows, grades, and credits. There is also a hidden or informal curriculum that surrounds teachers. How work is organized within schools; how teachers, students, administrators, and other personnel interact with one another; what behaviors are modeled by veterans; and how rewards and punishments are dispensed send powerful messages to the novice about where the boundaries of appropriate behavior lie and what the appropriate ways of understanding teaching and the responsibilities of teachers are. The pressures to conform, although usually subtle, are considerable and ever-present. Novice insecurity and vulnerability, along with anxiety about fitting in, add to the pressure to conform, even as points of contention between personal and institutional values begin to emerge and seek expression. The informal curriculum sent numerous messages to Kerrie about the nature of teachers and of teaching. Consider these messages in the light of the values of professionalism: expertise, judgment, autonomy, and collegiality.

Expertise

We begin with a message sent to Kerrie about her expertise. From time to time opportunities to be involved in a variety of professional activities outside of the classroom arose. One such opportunity left a particularly sour feeling: She was offered the possibility of earning some extra money by participating in a curriculum development project, which on the surface appeared to be an interesting and challenging activity. Unfortunately, the task turned out to be nothing more than going through textbooks and coding the assignments within them to the district outcomes-based education program. She was insulted and angry: Do "you know what they want us to do?! Take our English books and take a little card, like a 3×5 card, and with a paper clip attach one to every page that has a lesson on it [noting] which one [of the district's objectives] it fulfills. Would you do that?! That is busy work!"

Sometimes Kerrie wondered if baby-sitting was the most valued form of teacher expertise. For example, administrators occasionally canceled classes for whole-school activities. While she agreed with the general aim of "Spirit Week" — to encourage students to identify with the school — she found it irritating that class would be canceled for a football game between a few boys representing two different grade levels. "Who thinks they have the right to take away my period of academic teaching?" she complained. But just as irritating was the realization that during these times she would be relegated to the position of babysitter: "I was hired to teach these kids. I have to go out and [supervise them]. That makes me mad. That's a waste of my time. I don't want to baby-sit, I hate that!"

Moreover, it seemed as though the enhancement of Kerrie's expertise was seen as being of little consequence to anyone within the school. This message was carried in numerous ways: The team leader's failure to inform her of some of the school's policies had this effect: "You just find out [what is going on in the school] as you go . . . I feel like a lot of these things are the obligation of the team leader [to communicate]. *You are literally dropped into this system?* 'And you start swimming!'" Because Kerrie was not drowning during those early months, she received little attention from the administrators. The lack of attention surprised and frustrated her, although initially, feeling somewhat insecure, she rather liked being left alone. For example, when she was hired she was told by the principal that it was a district policy that she take 10 hours of inservice training, to be offered within the school, to help her through the year. Nothing was done, and at year's end she discovered she had simply been given the 10 hours credit; she would have preferred the courses and the attention. Ironically, the school had on-line a peer evaluation system as part of a career ladder program. By mid-year, Kerrie was quite interested in receiving feedback on her teaching, but discovered that she could not participate in the career ladder program until she had been teaching for three years; therefore she was effectively barred from taking advantage of the learning opportunities that would have come from being evaluated by a trained observer: "I'm not allowed to [be part of the program]. I'm probationary, I'm still a juvenile, get with it!"

Judgment

Numerous messages were sent about the value of teacher judgment. The general message was that many decisions, such as which classes would be taught, and which students would be assigned to these classes, were for the most part outside the purview of teachers and best made by administrators:

> There's another new kid that I have in the morning class who has moved up from the sixth grade. He's a seventh grader who was held back last year. Now he's been brought back up because he was still failing, so why not let him fail seventh grade instead of sixth grade twice [they reasoned]? Guess who got him? Bleeding heart. *Did anyone ask you if you wanted him?* They asked as though saying, "Do you want to have a bath as you are stripping this child and putting him in the tub?" It's that kind of asking.

Kerrie did not feel she could question the decision; instead she accepted it, and the student, unhappily. There may have been very good reasons for placing the child in Kerrie's class—certainly there are very good reasons, grounded in educational research, for arguing against holding children back; nevertheless, Kerrie was excluded from participating in such a conversation. On the positive side, during Kerrie's second year of teaching she had some influence over how the students were grouped within the core.

Autonomy

Messages were also sent about teacher autonomy and the need for administrators to maintain close supervision over teachers. A general message sent was that teachers needed to be policed; the implication was that they could not be trusted fully. Being policed by administrators was taken for granted as part of life within Rocky Mountain Junior High School, although none of the teachers liked it. Kerrie's first encounter with faculty dissent came as a result of the principal's practice, noted earlier, of placing notes in teachers' boxes calling attention to inappropriate behavior. Some of the notes were especially irritating: "One teacher got one that said, 'You left four minutes early!'" The teachers took their grievance to the Faculty Advisory Committee, which was composed of the building union representatives, a faculty member elected at large, the principal, and a vice principal. "People complained and said, 'We don't want notes in our boxes . . . if it's that petty, don't tell us. If it's big, tell us.'" The principal's response was to inform the teachers that he kept a file on each of them and that he gave them the notes to let them know what went into it: "This is to protect you," he said. Kerrie understood and sympathized with the principal's position: "Well, he's got to cover his ass, too. That's the thing, he's just doing his job."

The greater worth of bureaucracy and administration over instruction was communicated in other ways as well. For example, counselors and vice principals thought little of interrupting class with notes or requests to see students. In response, Kerrie eventually learned how to put these interruptions off. The librarian, in contrast, would wait until a natural break in instruction occurred before speaking to Kerrie.

Respect flows to those who are professional. Unfortunately, teachers enjoy far too little respect even within schools. For example, it was decided that in order to catch sluffers — perpetrators of a heinous crime, since funding was determined by an attendance-driven formula — a policy was instituted of rewarding a teacher with a candy bar for each sluffer caught.

> *They are offering candy bars to teachers!?* To teachers who catch [sluffers]. Which . . . means that you take an accurate roll every day to make sure the person is not on the absentee list, then make sure the next day they didn't check in. *Then you turn them in?* Yes. Then turn them in and get [the candy bar]. (pause). I don't have any yet.

Kerrie had no intention of participating, and, more important, she found the message sent about teachers a trifle disturbing: From the perspective of the administrators, the teachers had much in common with the students; both needed policing and both responded to childish rewards.

Unfortunately, Kerrie saw around her a few examples of teacher incompetence that forced her to conclude that maybe the administrators were correct in their assessment that teachers were in need of external policing. There was, for instance, a "reject from another school" across the hallway from Kerrie's room who frequently left his classes unattended; sometimes he even slept. She also was amazed at the general teacher response to the principal's announcement that the school's spelling test scores were "very low": Few teachers seemed to care. And it disturbed her to walk down the hallway and glance into a classroom to find "every kid . . . sitting . . . with a book, snoring, while one kid is reading aloud. That's not quality teaching to me!"

Collegiality

To Kerrie, as a newcomer, the staff appeared to be "cliquey" and divided; collegiality was little in evidence: "I wish everybody went to the lunchroom to eat lunch," she said. "I wish all the teachers went.

Then, it's like a party. But everyone gets cliquey, because you're seg-
mented kind of in the building itself. Like, for example, I don't even
know where the math rooms are. I just don't know where they are.
People don't really talk to each other that much. It really bothers me."
Some of the divisiveness was tied to association membership: Some
teachers joined the more recently organized American Federation of
Teachers (AFT) affiliate, which aggressively pressed issues related to low
salaries and the improvement of work conditions but which suffered
from a taint of trade unionism. Others joined the more conservative and
well established National Education Association (NEA) affiliate, which
suffered from the perception that it had done little over the years to
improve the working conditions of teachers and from a perception of
having incompetent leadership. Still others refused, often for monetary
reasons, to join either the AFT or NEA affiliate. Nonmembers were
viewed scornfully by both groups, even as they battled one another for
membership and power within the school and district.

These were not, of course, the only messages Kerrie received. Some
parents, and many students, let her know in various ways that what she
was doing was valued and respected. The principal, too, sent positive
messages about her personally. But the message sent about teaching,
separate from herself as a teacher, was that it was decidedly not a
profession. She was excluded from decisions profoundly affecting her
work life, was required to engage in menial tasks, and enjoyed autonomy only within the classroom and at the expense of isolation from other
adults within the building.

Kerrie considered all of these factors and seemed to be wondering,
did teachers deserve to be considered professionals? Could they be? She
answered this question personally: Others might not behave professionally, but she would to the best of her ability despite the limitations
placed on her by life within the school. What was at stake, in addition
to her pride and self-respect, was the learning of her students; the more
professional she became — the more skilled at managing complexity and
solving practical problems — she thought, the more likely they would
learn. She wanted badly to be the "one teacher in the lives [of her
students] who is different, [who cares about learning]. Why not let it be
me?" she asked. "Then why not have me be followed by 20 other [caring]
teachers through the rest of their schooling?" At year's end, by having
gradually come to know a number of teachers throughout the building,
she discovered, happily, that she was far from alone in this ambition;
there were several other teachers within the building who were, in
Kerrie's estimation, striving to be professional.

CHANGING IMAGES OF A TEACHER

Mother Figure

Kerrie began the year with a teacher identity closely tied to her mothering experience; she was a nurturer, a loving, fun, mother figure. Part of being a mother was to model virtue: "I always just thought it was every teacher's responsibility to [serve as a model of decency]. I guess I think everyone should do that, it's part of their job. Aren't we supposed to be . . . pillars of the community? That's what I've always said." Part of being a mother was to do the work without complaining, to be a steadying influence, and to give without taking: *Why did you expect to [spend money on your classes?] Is it just part of the job?* "That's how I've always seen it. I really didn't have any expectations except to buy the things I thought I would need." Another part was to create a warm, loving, secure environment within which young people could learn and develop.

Disciplinarian

As the year progressed, however, Kerrie's understanding of herself and the teaching role changed. Some of these changes came as a result of having to negotiate a place within the institution and finding the compromises required not wholly to her liking.

> November 11: *Has your role changed, the way you see yourself as a teacher?* I would say it's filling out. Things get added in. (pause). I don't even know how to say what's filling out, or anything about it. It's hard to say. I guess I see myself more as a disciplinarian than I had before [for one thing]. There's just . . . more coming into it, it's getting to be a harder (more complicated) job.

The language Kerrie used at different points throughout the year suggests a sequence to the "filling out" of her role. An important part of this filling out was that changes in her self-understanding were reflected in changes in how she interacted with and related to others on the faculty and to parents. The sequence seemed to go like this, beginning with the key image of teacher–mother, which persisted: teacher–mother, "community pillar," "bitch," "policewoman," "supervisor," and eventually, orchestra "director," instructional "leader," and member of a professional community.

"Bitch," "policewoman," and "supervisor" were unhappy images associated with the survival stage of teaching when Kerrie struggled to get a handle on classroom control and management while teaching some-one else's program. This was a time when other cherished values were temporarily shoved aside somewhat, with the result that she experi-enced considerable frustration and disappointment. Ultimately she dis-covered she could not be a bitch, a policewoman, or supervisor, especial-ly not full-time. Kerrie was not happy during those weeks of struggle. During an interview in late September, she remarked, for example: "I am kind of unhappy, I feel like a supervisor, not a teacher, too much [of the time]. I'm not in on any of the planning. It's not personal to me, this unit, it's totally impersonal." Kerrie felt disengaged and disconnected from the students and from the curriculum being taught. The role she was occupying fit poorly, uncomfortably.

Reaching Out

During this period Kerrie became heavily involved in inservice pro-grams offered through the district. As noted in Chapter 5, the courses helped her cope, but this was an unintended outcome. Initially she took them hoping to enrich her curriculum, improve her teaching skills, and accumulate credits toward salary increases. But, in addition, through the courses she began to link up with a wider educational community from which she gained useful ideas about curriculum and instruction, and, perhaps more significant, an increased awareness of the impor-tance of other teachers to her own development as a teacher. Through-out the year she continued taking these courses on a wide variety of topics, from state history to the instructional uses of newspapers. These relationships placed in stark relief the lack of collegiality she felt in Rocky Mountain Junior High School: *Do you feel any collegiality, esprit de corps?* "No, not really." In addition, Kerrie began to be involved, tangentially, in her professional association, first by attending meetings and later by speaking up and expressing her opinions. This involvement was a reflection of a growing self-confidence that manifested itself, among other ways, in her willingness to reject and reshape portions of the curriculum she had inherited. At these meetings she struck a friend-ship with the president of the NEA affiliate, which led to greater in-volvement in issues.

It was near the close of Kerrie's survival stage that she began to express an interest in spending some time in other teachers' classrooms and in becoming more involved with teachers in the school. She felt secure enough to begin reaching out of the classroom and its isolation. For this to happen, she would necessarily have to come to grips with some fears, as well as her own tendency to be a loner:

Would you want to be able to spend time in other people's classes? Yes, not a lot of time. *You could do that in your planning period.* Yes. I always wonder, would they want someone to come in and watch them? Why don't I? I would have time if I really wanted to. Partially because I'm really too chicken to go and ask them. OK, those I'd really want to watch the most would be the other core, and [a teacher I've been told is very good]. *So, part of what I hear you saying, when you say "chicken," is that there is an invasion of privacy that takes place.* Partially. Another thing is that I do get to watch someone teach all day [the team leader] . . . that really makes a difference.

Last question. You said you . . . kind of like to be alone, and your support group isn't here [at the school]; nevertheless, as you project your-self into the future, you'd like more strokes, more adult feedback. There seems to be kind of a contradiction there. I guess because I'm a loner, but I still want some professional [feedback]. Part of that, the part you are asking about, being isolated, has to do with my personality; [I like to be alone]. But wanting the professional help—which is the other side of what we've been talking about—I would have to put my personality away in order to get that, which I would do. *So, it's not that you want friends to come in.* No, it's professional help, I would say.

Kerrie was not alone in wishing for greater professional interaction and involvement. Indeed, within the building, and within teaching generally, teachers express this desire. Kerrie's situation was hardly unique; she was isolated, like other teachers, even though she was a member of an instructional team. John Goodlad notes in *A Place Called School* (1984), for example, that in the schools studied there were "little . . . data to suggest active, ongoing exchanges of ideas and practices across schools, between groups of teachers, or between individuals even in the same schools. Teachers rarely worked together on schoolwide problems." Moreover, "teacher-to-teacher links for mutual assistance in teaching or collaborative school improvement were weak or nonexistent, especially in the senior high schools." This said, Goodlad found that teachers wanted greater involvement and more interaction. Indeed, approximately three-fourths of the teachers sampled "indicated that they would like to observe other teachers at work" (pp. 187–88). Within Rocky Mountain Junior High School the problem was similarly wide-spread, as indicated by the results of a faculty survey administered in the late fall of Kerrie's second year of teaching. Despite it being a "good school," the majority of the faculty responding thought they received either "much too little" or "too little" praise from other teachers "for work done in class." Two-thirds reported feeling unappreciated and not particularly happy working within the school.

Instructional Leader

As Kerrie moved out of the survival stage of teaching, her teacher–mother image had broadened; for example, she would be more of a disciplinarian. The broadening continued in a line connected with a movement out of self and classroom, and toward others. The instructional leader and community member images arose, and expanded as she began to form professional links through inservice classes. Ultimately, these images blossomed as a result of a rather remarkable event: Near year's end, and partially as a result of reaching outward to make connections within the faculty, Kerrie was elected to be the NEA building representative. On the surface, however, her election seemed to represent an abrogation of responsibility on the part of the more senior members of the faculty, yet another indication of a lack of professionalism:

> Actually, one of the ladies who has [been the representative this year] asked me [if I was] interested in the union. I said, "Well, yes," because I've been kind of close with her, with what she has had to do this year. She asked if I would be upset if I were nominated. I said, "No, not really. I wouldn't mind doing it."

Kerrie found it somewhat flattering to have been asked, but, in retrospect, she saw her election in a slightly less favorable light: "Basically, they got me because everyone else in the school has done it except the first-year teachers." *Is it viewed as an unpleasant task to stick someone with?* "I don't think unpleasant. It's just who is going to volunteer to do more [than the minimum amount of work]." Just before the election, she doubted the wisdom of her decision, wondering what she had gotten herself into, but soon it was too late: "I was voted in. I didn't have the nerve to stand up and say, 'I won't do it.'" The evening of the election she attended an inservice workshop with a number of teachers who complained bitterly about various problems of teaching. Their complaints, which were troubling, helped put the election into a different light: "After [my workshop] last night, I just thought . . . boy, are we ever a nation of complainers here. I was really disgusted [and I want to do something more than complain]." Kerrie took her nomination and election as an opportunity to become fully involved within the building and the association, a natural step in her developing sense of professionalism: "I just feel like I've made pretty good progress this year in handling things in class. It's a good way to learn more about [teaching], to learn something more [about the profession]. Jump right in. Right?"

Unfortunately, like some of her early-year experiences with other teachers, her first experience as building representative was disappointing: For some reason, she was not informed of the first meeting, an orientation meeting for new representatives, until after it had been held.

Any further word about . . . the building representative job? Well, I found out that they forgot to tell me I was supposed to go to a meeting. *Who are they?* [The current representatives,] the people who are this year's reps. [It was] an orientation meeting. Rather important thing—don't you think?—that they maybe should have told me about? I think I probably should have received an invitation to it from the district, or from the union. You might.

Despite her irritation, she immediately got even more deeply involved, becoming chair of an association public relations committee, an opportunity that arose because she had become friendly with the district NEA president at association meetings.

[In addition, I've been selected to be the] chair . . . of some screwball committee next year. They just called me up and asked me to be president-elect. *Why in the world would you agree to do that?* Well, it's a new challenge. I'm not very good [at saying no]. *But you'll do it.* Yes. She told me pretty much what the job was. It's like producing a newspaper, a newsletter, or something. The newspaper is already done by someone. She's been doing it for several years. It's not as much [work] as it seems, I sure hope.
   Then the other question, why were you chosen? [This year's president] recommended me because I've had a lot of talks with her. She is this year's [district association] president. We're friends. *Why have you been talking to her?* Just at [association] meetings. She's come to the school to talk. They travel around and do PR. *But, aren't you supposed to hide in the back of the room and keep your head down?* I was a first-year teacher, and no one told me that! (laughter). [The team leader] would have said hide in the back of the room and keep your head down. *So, you have made yourself visible almost unintentionally?* Yes. *In order to be friendly?* I was just being me, and look what happened.

EMERGING PROFESSIONALISM

As Kerrie worked within the school and the association, she formed a vision of what it was to be professional, a vision she held as a standard for herself as well as for other teachers. This vision speaks to questions of autonomy only indirectly, but it relates directly to teacher expertise, judgment, and collegiality. In addition, her vision raised ethical issues about the personal qualities that should be evidenced by those who work with young people. For Kerrie, the central criterion of professionalism was involvement in the larger educational community in order to strengthen it:

> To me, part of being a professional is finding out [what research] is being done, talking to other [teachers], joining an association—one or the other. Getting involved so you know what the issues are. [If teachers are involved] then they have all the right in the world to complain, [but they should] at least work on changing things.

In addition, Kerrie believed professionals subscribe to professional journals, as she did; "help other teachers out"; and take classes, "like the classes I'm taking. They help me so much. That's part of my professionalism . . . engaging in those so I can do better or just expand myself — do what's right for the kids." And they engage in evaluation of one another. She described the characteristics of a professional teacher within the classroom in this way: "Someone who does a good job, who does their best job, and who is always changing to make it better. Someone who is fair to the kids. And, in their own way, loving. You can see teachers who are really strict, [for example,] but underneath that you see the love."

Kerrie's understanding of professionalism placed the vast majority of the burden on the individual teacher to behave professionally. For the most part, she seemed to accept the institution as given, believing that within it there was sufficient room for her to work out her own role definition and that there were useful mechanisms for bringing about change where change was necessary, despite the "unprofessional" ways in which teachers were viewed and treated. Her message seemed to be, act professionally and you will be treated professionally. At the same time, she accepted some limitations on the possibility of change as inevitable reflections of life within massive bureaucracies: Thus, her empathy for the principal's position. Some things she would just have to live with. The association enjoyed a prominent place within her vision as perhaps the central means by which to forge work conditions more nearly in line with her desires. Yet, again, she recognized and accepted limitations on the association's power. For example, two issues that gnawed at her were low pay and large class size, neither of which she thought the association would have any influence over changing.

It is unclear where Kerrie's involvement within the larger educational community will lead. Organizationally, she rapidly moved up through working on various committees and by the high quality of her service. By becoming association building representative and by serving on the Faculty Advisory Committee, she became a key player in building politics, a member of the "inner group." But her efforts were not to push a particular vision of professionalism, for example, greater autonomy and more influence over curriculum decisions. Rather, her aim first and foremost was to make the institution a more pleasant, supportive, and interesting place within which to work. Just as her images of self as teacher evolved, so will her views of professionalism. For now, it is involvement that matters most. With increased involvement have come some significant changes in Kerrie's feeling about herself and especially about her work in the school. In an interview conducted during the late fall of her second year of teaching, she put it this way: *What is really satisfying about this [as compared with last year]? What stands out?* "Comraderie. Working with other teachers. Getting to know more teachers. Having more of a friendship and more of a working relationship [with them]." This is no small accomplishment.

QUESTIONS FOR CONSIDERATION

1. When you think of a professional, what images come to mind? What is it about professionals that you respect?
2. Given your view of professionalism, think back and consider the teachers you studied with as a student. Do you think of any of them as having been professional? What separated these teachers from those you believe not to have been professional?
3. Consider your personal values and inclinations. Given a situation similar to Kerrie's (isolation, limited support), what would you have done? Would you have withdrawn further into the classroom or perhaps have gotten involved more fully within the school? What options seem most sensible to you?

ACTIVITIES

1. Speak with a teacher you respect. Does he or she believe professionalism is important to educational reform? Does he or she think progress is being made toward achieving this goal? Ask if the teacher is a member of an association? Ask his or her opinion of the association's effectiveness in furthering professionalism among teachers.
2. Call the local teacher associations and ask specifically what they are

doing to further teacher autonomy, expertise, collegiality, and respect. Let the association representatives know your views on these issues.

3. Obtain a copy of the education bills passed during the most recent state legislative session (typically these are provided free of charge). Review the bills in the light of their likely influence on the development of teacher professionalism. Do the bills represent reason for being optimistic about the future of teacher professionalism, or are they a cause for concern?

4. Kerrie placed a very high value on involvement within the education community. If you are teaching, speak with other teachers about the opportunities available for becoming involved. Especially, try to find out if teacher support groups are available that embrace the enhancement of teacher professionalism as an ideal. Consider carefully the desirability of becoming involved in such a group or, if one is not available, of forming one. If you are not teaching, but are involved in a teacher education program, call the district office to locate a school that is thought to be actively promoting teacher professionalism. Set up an appointment with the principal, vice principal, teacher leader, or someone else who is actively engaged in the effort, for the purpose of discussing specifically what is being done and with what results. Seek to understand what is working within the school and why it is working.

7   The Second Year

A Refinement of the First

The foundation and walls for Kerrie's second year of teaching were provided by the first, which is not surprising. For teachers generally, each year of teaching builds on the previous year; they rarely begin a year without drawing on their experiences of the year before, unless they are facing a new teaching assignment (Clark & Yinger, 1987). Having built an instructional edifice, the second year gave Kerrie the opportunity to refine it where she liked the design and to recreate it where she did not. Now, having a basis for comparison, she became increasingly reflective about practice, with impressive results; she was firmly established within the mastery stage.

DESCRIPTION FROM SECOND-YEAR OBSERVATION

To situate the discussion of the second year, a rather lengthy description taken from observation notes follows, about two class periods on the same October day after a four-day weekend as was described at the beginning of Chapter 5, but a year later. Just as on that first October day, the students were wild, difficult to settle down and get working. From her previous year's experience, Kerrie anticipated this in her planning for both instruction and management. For example, she began each class with a whole-group, teacher-directed activity as a means of settling the students down and focusing their attention, and she monitored their behavior very closely. Clearly, it was a very different teacher who met the challenge of that October day in the second year from the one who faced it in the first. Over the course of the year Kerrie had developed the teaching skills and understandings necessary to turn a potentially disastrous day into a productive learning experience. In particular, readers will note the presence of several of the skills discussed in Chapters 3 and 4 related to classroom discipline and management: with-it-ness, a brisk pace, and clear transitions between activities, among others.

English Class

Kerrie stands by the door ushering students into the room. Some kid with her.

10:02: The buzzer sounds. The students are very excited; all but two are in their seats. "ok. Get out a piece of paper." Kerrie shushes them as she passes out the spelling lists for the week.

10:04: "The first word is 'debtor'—a debtor is someone who owes a debt." Silence. The students are writing as she talks: first the word from the list, then the definition. "Second word, 'municipal'. . . . " It's a very rapid pace. "Write quickly," Kerrie tells the students. "Are you writing these down, Vern?" "Yes." "Number five is 'pension,' retirement money, when you are old and living off a pension, retirement money."

10:09: "Number eight, 'coincide,' two things that happen at the same time." The students are writing. A little whispering can be heard. Looking at the offenders, Kerrie remarks, "I'm not going to go back and tell you what they are—shush."

10:11: "Number fifteen, 'legible,' clear enough to be read."

10:13: All students are on-task but one. "Don, you need to move, go over there." "ok," and he moves quickly to a desk apart from the others.

10:17: "Last word, 'vertical.'" Drawing on the social studies simulation, Galleons, being done in the next class period which will run throughout the quarter, she asks, "Can anyone tell me which is vertical? Longitude or latitude?" Student: "Longitude." "Very good." As the student gives the answer, Kerrie begins passing out an assignment the purpose of which is to get the students working with the words by producing different word forms. "ok, we are going to do the first part of the assignment together. Oh! Thank you, Mrs. B," Kerrie says laughing, "for doing my work!" "The first word was 'debtor.'" Student: "debt." "The next word is what?" "Depart," a student volunteers, and almost immediately a second student interjects, "departure." "Very good." "ok, what could we do with the next word?"

"Chas, did you throw anything?" "No." She lets it go (no clear evidence).

The students work on the assignment.

Kerrie circulates the room helping students. While circulating, she sees Chas throw a piece of paper and warns him not to do it again.

10:32: The students appear nearly finished. Another quick transition (a third spelling activity). Standing in front of the room, she calls the students to focus their attention on her: "This is a hard but fun activity," she says. "What is an antonym?" Kerrie describes the task, demonstrates on the board, and gets the students to work.

10:35: "Chas," Kerrie says without any anger, "pick up your stuff, out into the hall, I'm writing a referral for you." As he gets up to leave, without protest, she waves goodbye while the other students seem to work with additional urgency. She keeps circulating and helping the other students. Kerrie pauses, then writes a referral and walks out into the hall and gives it to Chas, who immediately leaves for the office. [After the period ended, Kerrie was asked what happened to warrant a referral. She said she had given him two warnings to stop throwing things; the third incident necessitated a referral.]

10:40: Kerrie circulates as the students raise their hands for help. They are busily working. There is a little low, task-related talk.

10:43: Kerrie is still moving quickly from student to student helping them and giving suggestions: "Jeopardize means to put into danger; so, what is the opposite of jeopardize?" The student gives a word and Kerrie says, "Yes," and moves on. Some students are helping one another.

10:48: The students are still working. One student approaches Kerrie and asks if she can recite the poem she has memorized (a means of obtaining extra credit). The student recites while Kerrie keeps an eye on the rest of the class.

10:49: The students are still working. Kerrie reminds them of when the assignment is due.

10:50: Buzzer. She dismisses them.

Social Studies Class

Kerrie goes to the door and monitors students in the hallway and as they enter her classroom. She greets some of them playfully as they come in. The one-minute warning buzzer sounds.

10:55: The tardy buzzer sounds. All the students are in their seats. "ok, I'm passing back your social studies maps. Start on them immediately." The seats are arranged in groups of six to facilitate the simulation: Each cluster represents the crew of one ship. Each crew is competing with the other crews, as part of the explorers unit, to be the first to sail to the New World and back. Movement comes by virtue of work done and is indicated by periodically moving ships on a large map of the world tacked to the back wall of the classroom.

"ok, we have work to do when you are through with your map assignment, so get busy, but do a good job. A number of you have been getting wrong answers." She then reminds them, again, of the task and how to do it. "Shush, get busy. I see you talking, you guys may move backward!" (This was a slight threat: Bad behavior on the part of a crew could result in their ship losing ground in the race to the New World and home again.)

11:00: Most of the students are on-task. A few are talking. To these she says (reminding them of the incident last period with Chas), "I want you to know I have my referrals on my desk; you *too* can visit the office." She says this in an almost friendly way: not a threat, just a reminder.

11:01: Kerrie warns against copying: "You might get the wrong answers."

11:02: Kerrie helps a student who was absent on the previous day. She explains the assignment. While she is helping this student, three others who need help begin to gather around.

11:05: Still circulating. One student starts to get rowdy: "Craig, you can sit in the hall, it's fine with me." He gets the message and settles down.

While rushing to help students, "If it were I and I was through, I'd go back to make certain I didn't have North and West mixed up." (She made this comment because she noted it as a problem for one student and thought others might have made the same error.)

11:10: Moving quickly. While moving through the aisles, Kerrie overhears a student giving an answer to another student. She stops, crouches down to his level and says, "That is wrong, you just shared a wrong answer." While helping another student, she says to the class, "When you're through, you should be reading. Craig (who is often off-task and disruptive) sit down, you're not halfway through." "I know that." Another student, presumably one of his fellow crew members, begins to help Craig.

11:12: Students are finishing at different times. "Are you finished, Dawn Ann?" "Yes." "I want to see your paper," which she quickly reviews.

11:13: Kerrie sits down next to Craig to help him.

11:14: Back to moving quickly from student to student as they raise their hands. She engages each at their own level, eye to eye. "You guys [who have finished] should be reading, you should always bring a book." (The students had a reading assignment of 1000 pages per term. Any free time they had was supposed to be spent working on this assignment.) "Remember, your map must be finished today or your group will get a zero."

11:16: Kerrie collects the maps. "ok, get out a piece of paper; we will be moving into our next [topic] — get out a piece of paper, now." Using an overhead projector she introduces the topic: "Write down everything I write, this is an outline. We're going to start talking about a time called the 'Dark Ages.'" A brief overview of the time follows, focusing particularly on how people lived:

"Dark Ages": 476 AD to 1000 AD

1. Few comforts of life
2. Food — plain, spoiled
3. Clothes — uncomfortable
4. Crude houses
5. Little learning

11:27: A person from the office interrupts class for the second time. Craig pulled out of class. The lecture continues.

11:35: "OK, that's as far as we're going to go today. We still have a little time." She goes through a list of activities that the students should be working on. "Some of you are missing assignments, look over there." (She has a large sheet on the wall that lists all the students and all the assignments. Marks are made alongside the students' names as work is completed.)

11:40: Students working.

11:44: "We have two VIPs for people working quietly, Dolores and Annetta." Buzzer. She dismisses class.

PLANNING

Curriculum

Teachers engage in several different kinds of planning, of which yearly or long-range, unit, weekly, and daily are most important for understanding Kerrie's second year of teaching (Clark & Yinger, 1987). Kerrie focused primarily on yearly and unit planning during the late spring and summer between her first and second years of teaching. She was ready for school a few weeks before it began: "By the second week of August I was really starting to get anxious [for school to begin]. I am so excited for school to start." She began, once again, filling out a calendar, but this time she had a solid basis for her decisions; there was far less guesswork. In planning for the new year she thought carefully about what she had done the first year. Her preparation for the reading program, which would run all year, provides a good illustration of this process:

> They didn't read that much [last year]. I didn't feel like [they did enough].
> Too many kids hate to read, they aren't good [enough] at it [so they can]

just sit down and read. It's like writing, or playing the piano, you have to do it to get better. There wasn't enough. [Mostly] in class I read to them. Now, that's great as a role model and so that they can see how interesting things can be. But it doesn't help their reading skills any. So, I've decided they have to read 1000 pages a quarter and it's going to be half of their reading grade. They have to, for example, at some point during the first quarter . . . read a Newbery book. They'll have to fill out brief written reports . . . that's how I'm going to keep track of how many pages they've read. Every Friday I'll ask how many pages they've read [to help pace them].

Setting up her reading program in this way had the advantage of addressing another of the disappointments from the first year:

Who is going to read all these book reports? Me. That's part of what I want to do. Remember, I said last year I felt they weren't writing enough? I spent time on other things last year. Now, I think I should be making them do more writing and, thereby, force myself to read more. It just has to be that way [if their writing is to improve]. I feel like they were cheated last year in what they did.

The time necessary to do the extra reading would be available because less time would have to be spent in other ways: "I was still planning [throughout last year]. Now, I'm mostly planned for the whole year. So, I feel like I have more time [available]." Time would also become available because of her increasing efficiency. For example, she would "utilize [seat-work time] better." But, if she could not make sufficient time in these ways to read the students' writing, she vowed to do a bit more work at home, which she did: "I have been doing it at home," she said during the third week of school. "I read a lot of them yesterday in school, [though]. I'm just faster at preparing and I'm trying to grade faster, as well."

She began planning units by reviewing the files of activities and assignments accumulated during the first year. Based on her recollection of how successful the units were, adjustments were made in sequence, and some topics and activities were added or deleted. The outcome of this review was an outline of what would be done over a week or two. Actual lesson planning involved very little writing; mostly it was a mental process followed by a brief period of time gathering and organizing materials: "I plan in my brain, kind of."

Management

Unlike her preparation for her first year of teaching, this time she planned carefully for discipline and management.

What are you going to do about management? I'm starting out stricter, for one thing. For example, when the bell rings you're tardy if you're not sitting down in your seat.

You are going to remember that? I hope I am. This is why: I lost a lot of time, class time, last year waiting. That can add up to five minutes [wasted in each class]. I hope to cue better. For example, they would wait for me to say, "Alright, get out your papers." This year, I'm going to say, "When you come in and sit down, get ready for class. If we had an assignment yesterday, get it out. We're going to correct it. If you had an assignment and it's not finished, get it out and work on it. If you're all through, get out a book and read it." But, class has begun when the bell rings. [To help them learn this] I will stay on them all the time. Repetition . . . being ready [myself when the bell rings]. Not still messing around getting things ready.

In addition, like the year before, she carefully prepared the classroom for the arrival of the students, beginning with seating. "I turned my classroom sideways this time . . . so their backs [will be] toward that kind of hall." She did this, wisely, to minimize distractions from the other class areas. She also planned to have assigned seating and seating charts in order to more quickly learn the students' names and to spot problem areas.

In addition, based on her experience, she decided to make a concerted effort, especially at the beginning of the year, to better inform parents about what their children were doing and how well they were doing it. Indeed, through the first several weeks of school Kerrie called no fewer than two parents each evening, typically spending about fifteen minutes on the telephone.

I started [calling] because I had some kids right off who really had trouble. So, I felt like I needed to call just so they wouldn't get totally lost so soon. I have to deal with them, somehow. I really like parent/teacher conferences a lot. I've discovered that a phone call is just as good. I've been getting [very] positive feedback from . . . parents. Like, "Oh, I'm so glad you called. Not one teacher called me ever last year. He had so much trouble." I just . . . decided I'm going to call a couple of parents every night. It's really [having a] positive [effect on] what's happening in the classroom. I'm also going to call some parents for positive reasons. There are some kids who really deserve to have a teacher call and say [something good].

The First Day

Kerrie planned the first day of school carefully, to begin getting the students into the patterns of behavior she desired. As Kauchak and

Eggen (in press) note, the first day "sets the tone and lays the foundation for the rest of the days to follow."

> *Talk through what you are going to do [on the first day].* The buzzer sounds. It will be T. A. (teacher's advisory, or home room as it used to be called). First I want to assign lockers and get them taken care of. The short kids need a bottom locker. That kind of thing. See, I didn't even think about those things last year. That was trouble all through the year. Then we're going to go through folders that [the administration] gives us, a school folder that contains the rules of the school. We're going to talk about rules. I have a list sitting on my desk of things to go over that I want to say to them [about rules and procedures]. Bathroom procedures, like you cannot go to the bathroom! We also have to go over the exit route from the school [in case there's an emergency].
>
> Going through that should pretty much take all of T. A. Forty minutes, I suppose, by the time we get out to the lockers and back in.
>
> In my [regular] classes I have a disclosure statement that I will be passing out. [It will include my expectations For example,] if I expect good spelling in reading, I also expect it in social studies, that kind of thing. What the grade breakdown is like. Things like that. [I'll also tell them, like the students in T. A., my rules and procedures,] like being in [their seats] when the bell rings, or [it counts as] tardy.

Following her review of rules, policies, and procedures, Kerrie planned to go directly into a whole-group activity. For the first class the assignment would be from a reading magazine. While the students worked on the assignment, the plan was for her team to meet and to make certain the students were where they should be.

These were her plans for the first day; however, all did not go as intended.

7:53: Warning buzzer. The students brave the door and begin filtering in. Kerrie walks along the rows with a seating chart calling out students' names. They move to the assigned seats without protest.

7:55: Students are silent in anticipation. Kerrie comments as she begins to read the roll: "Tell me if you want to go by something else."

7:58: "The first thing we need to do is locker assignments. Is there anyone who must have a lower locker? Jerry (a handicapped boy), OK."

7:59: A welcome from the vice principal comes over the intercom.

8:04: The announcements from the office are still going: "This is the warning of a fire drill . . . BZZZZ!! Next we will demonstrate the sound of an earthquake warning. Please remember these sounds."

T. A. unfolded just as Kerrie had intended; there were no surprises.

In a friendly but businesslike manner she reviewed the policies, procedures, and rules that would govern her classes. Just prior to the final buzzer, she said: "Also, you are not excused [from class] until I excuse you. If you are noisy, say for three minutes, I will hold you for three minutes after class." The buzzer sounded and the students jumped up to leave: "ok, since you decided to leave, you may come back [and sit quietly] until I dismiss you." They returned. "ok, have a nice day." Kerrie did what she had said she would do prior to the beginning of school, "I [will] stay on them all the time." She would be "stricter" in order to create the fun but orderly classes she still sought.

The first period also began as planned: All the students were gathered in one area, and each teacher quickly called off the names of the students assigned to him or her: "ok. I'm Mrs. B., a third of you will go with me." The students were told to move swiftly to their classroom areas once their names were read.

8:38: "Welcome." Kerrie begins circulating a calendar and tells the students to put their birthdays on it, "quietly—I'm going to be talking. This is social studies. My name is Mrs. B. The way you remember to say it is this. . . . ok, when the bell rings you must be in your seat: If you are sharpening your pencil, you are tardy; if you are in someone else's seat, you are tardy. . . . When the bell rings, it is my time. ok, get out a piece of paper. It's the first day of class, you should have paper. I want you to write [these rules] down: 'Be in your seat or you are tardy.' The school policy is that you cannot leave the classroom to go to the bathroom, so it's my policy, too . . . same with drinks. You must be prepared every day—bring paper, pencils, books. ok, we need to talk about food. No pop. It's ok to eat some things as long as it doesn't [disturb] me. I also don't mind if you chew gum, I chew gum. Don't write on your desks, if your desk is dirty come and tell me or you will end up cleaning all the desks. Write this down. Roughhousing is an immediate referral, no discussion. No throwing—this is not basketball. Cheating—if I find you have a problem with cheating, I will have [the teacher in the other classroom] watch the class and you and I will march down to the office and you will call your parents while I stand there; it brings an automatic U (unsatisfactory citizenship). I'm assuming no spit wads."

"These (pointing to the board) are the things you need to bring [with you to class]." The list includes markers or pencils, small ruler, scissors (if possible), glue stick, crayons. "We'll be doing lots of fun things."

8:50: They practice the exit drill. "Very good, and so quietly," she says.

8:53: "Is the birthday list going around?" [For birthdays, Kerrie placed the student's name on the board, acknowledged the student, and gave him or her a Rocky Mountain Junior High School pencil, which the students liked receiving.]

As Kerrie was about to move into the next activity, she received a signal from one of the other teachers. There was a problem with how the students had been grouped. The classes were of very uneven size, and a large number of students had not been accounted for. Kerrie made the planned assignment and went into the area joining the classrooms to meet with the other teachers and try and sort out what had happened. Confusion followed.

9:00: The team leader: "We all either need to ability group, or not." Apparently there were at least two different rolls, one reflecting ability grouping and another reflecting more of a mix of students. Kerrie, speaking to the students: "When the bell rings you are not excused."
9:04: The bell rings. Kerrie: "You are not excused until I excuse you." The students return and sit down.
9:11: The teachers are still trying to figure out what to do as second period begins. "OK," they agree, "we're going to try this roll again," with unsatisfactory results.
9:26: Surprisingly, the students are patiently waiting, talking quietly, while the teachers are still trying to figure out what has happened.
9:30: The students are regrouped. Kerrie begins class all over again.

Minor grouping modifications continued throughout the first week. What should have been a reasonably quiet day, a time for getting organized, had just the opposite effect: Students and teachers were bewildered, wondering what was going on. Kerrie was concerned. Knowing that these first few days would set a tone for subsequent days, she resolved to quickly put the problem behind her and establish the order she desired. The source of the problem was simply poor communication between the team leader and the team: Grouping changes had been made without full knowledge and understanding of all the teachers involved, with the result that at least two different sets of class rolls existed and no one knew for certain who was in whose class. Moreover, team members disagreed over how the students should be assigned. A compromise of sorts emerged: Students were ability grouped in reading (with Kerrie being assigned two average groups), and were somewhat randomly mixed in English and social studies. "Listen. [One team member] wanted to have it the way we've got it. [The team leader] wanted to have them all ability grouped. I was caught in the middle. I can see both sides. But, [what's important to me is] to have one group of kids—

whether they're high, medium, or low — all the way through." Her opinion was ignored, and with it the core idea was seriously undermined. Nevertheless, once enrollments stabilized, Kerrie began the long process of "getting them into shape," as she put it.

INSTRUCTIONAL PATTERNS

As noted, an essential aspect of establishing and maintaining order — of getting the students in shape — as well as of establishing and maintaining a desirable learning climate, is to structure the environment, in particular through routines. Structure is also enhanced by the identification of appropriate patterns of instructional activity that are embedded within a framework of routines. A structured classroom environment lets the students know what is expected of them, how to behave, and what is coming up. Through structure the environment is made predictable and secure. But a classroom environment should not be too predictable: Between the extremes of rigidity and chaos are classes that are structured, yet flexible; predictable and orderly, yet varied and responsive to serendipity. Kerrie struggled during her first year of teaching to locate this spot between extremes; during her second year of teaching it was on this spot that she intended to homestead.

The progress Kerrie made in identifying and organizing appropriate learning activities was discussed in Chapters 3 and 4. The patterns established there were refined during the second year. A brief description follows of the daily pattern of activities for each of the three classes, along with the weekly instructional pattern where one existed.

Reading

Every reading class began with Kerrie, in front of the class, reading from a book she chose because of high student interest, quality (a number were Newbery winners), and occasionally fit with the content being addressed in social studies: "As soon as I walk up here with the book, they're quiet because they want to know what's going on [in it]. They shush each other." Slight instructional variations sometimes followed Kerrie's reading, but generally an assignment followed. Often she passed out short stories for the students to read that illustrated well one or another idea or concept being taught, such as theme, setting, or plot. A discussion of the short story and a written assignment or quiz would come next. Sometimes a dictionary assignment followed her reading. When time was left over, the students were expected to "free read" to accumulate pages toward the 1000 required per term. Every Friday she reminded them of how many pages they should have read to be caught up and urged them to keep reading.

This pattern was interrupted from time to time by special activities and sometimes units. For example, she allowed the students to read, in groups of six, novels chosen from a list she provided. In class, time was provided for the groups to read together (they chose how they would do this) and then to prepare a presentation to the class on the books. Class presentations were graded by the entire class based on criteria established by Kerrie: "The first group you are going to hear from [today] is *The Westing Game*. You are going to grade them [on their presentation]. Don't grade [the group] until they are through with their presentation. I am also going to be grading them." Just before the presentations began, Kerrie reminded the class: "The way an audience participates is that it is quiet through the performance and claps at the end." Plays, a reader's theatre, and illustrated stories followed.

English

For the most part, the content of English was established by the textbook. Typically, the students had work from the previous day, which at the buzzer they were to get out for correcting. Assignments were then exchanged "with a partner" and quickly corrected: "OK, three points on every sentence, hurry, so we can get started." Giving English assignments from the book was one way in which Kerrie provided for students who finished their work at different times: Those who did not complete their assignments finished them as homework. Once the previous day's assignment was corrected, Kerrie went over new material and made yet another seat-work assignment.

Such a pattern can easily become deadly, as you will recall from your own schooling. Kerrie was aware of the danger and periodically interrupted the pattern by planning departures; she too got bored. For example, based on her experience of the first year, she again planned a newspaper unit and early in the year had the students engage in a creative writing assignment.

Every Monday, Wednesday, and Friday the students had spelling. Monday Kerrie gave and defined a list of words, sometimes having the students help her with the definitions and with examples. An assignment followed requiring the use of the words, which would be corrected quickly in class the next day. Wednesday she gave a pretest followed by a brief assignment requiring the use of the words being studied, and writing misspelled words two or sometimes more times. Occasionally, on Thursdays she had a spelling bee or had the students play "spelling baseball" for review purposes. The spelling test was on Friday.

Social Studies

Social studies was the least patterned of the three classes Kerrie taught, which may account for its being the class with the highest rate of student off-task behavior. Perhaps it was for this reason that Kerrie frequently listed on the board and reviewed what the students were to be doing during the period. At the beginning of the year social studies started with whole-group activities, "because it's much easier to monitor." But by the Christmas break, other types of activities were slated first. What gave order to the diversity was the routinized way in which class always began—students had to be in their seats ready to receive instructions or else they would be marked tardy—and general reliance on activities to which the students were accustomed, ones like those used in English and reading.

Social studies followed a topical unit pattern. Kerrie would introduce a topic (e.g., "the Constitution," "the explorers") often with a brief lecture following an outline, which the students were to copy, projected from an overhead (as described at the beginning of this chapter). Through a variety of activities, games, puzzles, readings, worksheets, reports, art projects, plays, and simulations, the students would explore the topic in some detail. Frequently, in addition to the outline, units were given cohesiveness by ongoing projects such as a Constitution booklet to which a page was added to each day or the simulation, "Galleons," mentioned earlier.

The patterns described came about because of the experimentation of Kerrie's first year of teaching. For the most part, by the end of the first year she had identified all of the pieces that would eventually compose her instructional patterns, but it was only when coupled with a set of workable routines that they began to have the desired educational effect. To gain the kind of student behavior and classroom climate she desired, she would have to consistently reinforce the routines, which is precisely what she did.

CHANGING PERCEPTIONS OF STUDENTS

Increased knowledge of the students was an important element in the successes of Kerrie's second year, affecting virtually every aspect of teaching. Like the expert teachers described by Berliner (1986), she felt she knew the students even before meeting them and could anticipate the problems she would face: "At the beginning of last year I didn't know if a kid misbehaved what that was going to lead to. This year, I know what's going to happen." You may recall that just prior to the beginning of her first year of teaching Kerrie laughingly described her students as "know-it-all brats." She based this opinion on her experience as a mother and on her recollection of herself as a young person. This was, obviously, a very simpleminded view of young people, reflecting considerable naiveté and, perhaps, uncertainty. While lack of knowledge of the students was a critical source of many of Kerrie's problems, over the course of the year a rich understanding and appreciation of the students emerged, which greatly facilitated planning for both instruction and management as well as aided in the establishment of reasonable expectations. It also gave her perspective when activities failed, as when, for instance, the students resisted engaging in an unusual or creative assignment. She could shrug such problems off and maintain her resolve to produce a "fun" class: "You have to make it wonderful enough that they don't know it's medicine . . . I won't give up [doing some unusual things]."

Early in her second year of teaching, Kerrie briefly described a seventh grader this way:

It's a person who is trying to really get their act together. *What does that mean?* Not rely on parents so much. They've gotten the idea they've got to do things for themselves. [They're] maturing . . . [they worry about being] laughed at by . . . their friends. For some that is really important; [others] are still off in Rocket World, or something, the ozone. They're just so much caught in between [ages]. There are some kids who are totally undeveloped, physically, and others who are completely developed. Wearing makeup and with their hair ratted up to the ceiling. Others are just little clean kids still, little children. . . .

Peer pressure [is powerful]. They're academically pulled two different directions: They're still lazy little kids and yet they can . . . see the importance of education.

What do they value? A can of hairspray. Materialistic things, a lot. And yet they really care a lot about the feelings of other people in class, too—sometimes; sometimes they're really mean to each other, too. For example, . . . I had a girl come during the afternoon class who . . . said she was checking out. "I need to go home." This other girl said, "Look at that [ugly] headband she's got on." I chewed her out . . . I was so mad at her. "Do you think every girl was born with a pretty face?" She said, "Well, why are you so mad?" I said, "Because that is so mean, you don't care at all that you said that loud enough for her to hear." Some just don't have any feelings that way.

Last year you called them "know-it-all brats." I'd back off that . . . [although] sometimes I feel that way. Sometimes I think they're just trying too hard. . . .

As Kerrie's knowledge of the students increased, her affection for them deepened, which had a subtle but profound effect on the class-room climate. *You really like them, don't you?* "I do. I never thought I would, especially about five years ago. I have [empathy] for them." Most days there was a warmth and friendliness about the classroom, even while to the outside observer Kerrie was clearly in charge.

CONCLUSION

Although it began a bit raggedly, Kerrie's second year of teaching represented a dramatic improvement over the first. Consistency, confidence in the classroom, increased efficiency, humor, warmth, and flexibility are qualities that quickly come to mind when describing Kerrie during her second year of teaching. To be sure, she still was concerned about discipline and management problems from time to time, and she was frequently puzzled over problems of student motivation, but she was clearly on top of the situation and in control.

Perhaps the most striking change that took place was in how Kerrie generally approached problems: she was less reactive and more proactive. Put differently, she became much more reflective. Throughout the preceding chapters, Kerrie was described as engaging in halting experimentation and in trial-and-error approaches to problem solving in the classroom. Such approaches are inevitable given the uncertainty with which the novice begins teaching and the unfamiliarity of the environment. Such experimentation is not necessarily without direction, however. For Kerrie, purpose and direction came from her firm commitment to achieving a certain kind of learning climate, characterized as "fun" and "warm." When she tested a solution to a problem that was inconsistent with this aim, and therefore with her personal values, she would give it up after a time and continue experimenting (as when she adopted a program of Assertive Discipline, revised it, and then dropped it completely during the second year). Gradually, given the strength of her aims and increasing knowledge of herself, teaching, and the students, experimenting became more a matter of testing informed hypotheses — loosely conceived and based on a growing repertoire of skills and understandings — than of guesswork. As presented in the illustration of Kerrie's thinking about how to improve the students' reading and writing skills, she began to engage in a rather sophisticated and ongoing "reflective conversation" with the problems and materials of teaching

(Schon, 1987, p. 44). This conversation continued in the midst of teaching, just as it did, although in somewhat different form, during the interviews and at times when Kerrie could distance herself from immediately pressing events to plan ahead. With increased reflectivity came increased power within the classroom, and with increased power came a much improved learning program for the students. And when the students were learning as Kerrie intended, greater feelings of self-worth and professional satisfaction inevitably followed.

QUESTIONS FOR CONSIDERATION

1. Kerrie was a different teacher from the first to the second year. To what would you attribute her success?
2. Given the descriptions contained in this chapter, what further improvements would you hope to see in her teaching?
3. What are the strengths and weaknesses of Kerrie's approach to planning? How does her approach differ from your own?
4. Review Kerrie's instructional patterns for the three classes. Is she emphasizing the right learning outcomes? If not, what would you do differently and why? Are her patterns ones you would adopt yourself? Why or why not? If not, what would you do differently?
5. Despite Kerrie's planning for the first day of school, problems arose. What would you have done in her spot?
6. Kerrie is described as engaging in a substantial amount of trial-and-error testing of ideas. Will you engage in a similar process? If so, what will you do to avoid communicating to the students that you are wishy-washy and uncertain of what you are doing?

ACTIVITIES

1. Drawing on your experience, assess Kerrie's description of young people. How good or accurate is it? Write your own description of the students you are or will be teaching. How familiar are you with them? Do you know enough about them to be able to make reasonable instructional decisions? Consider how you might get to know the students in ways that will be useful for planning before actual instruction begins.
2. Make a written plan for the first day of school. Include in your plan a list of rules and the reasons why you think they are important, and plan to share it with the students. Are your reasons compeling? Ask a student of the appropriate age his or her opinion.

8 Problems of a Changing Context

Accountability, Mentoring, and Teacher Evaluation

Previous chapters have described the dramatic changes in Kerrie from the beginning of her first year to her second year of teaching. To complete the account of the year, it is necessary to discuss changes that took place in the work context. Small context changes may dramatically affect the quality of a teacher's professional life: complicating or simplifying it; debasing or ennobling it. In Kerrie's case, just when she began to think that smooth sailing was ahead, work within Rocky Mountain Junior High School changed, making teaching more difficult.

One change was that teaming was weakened. A teacher in the team who had been an occasional confidant transferred to another school and was replaced by a male 20-year veteran who had no interest whatsoever in working with other teachers. Moreover, the team leader was assigned a split core: She taught English and reading, but not social studies. And so the occasional team meetings of Kerrie's first year of teaching became almost nonexistent during her second year. The core concept (having one group of students for three periods) was shattered, as noted in Chapter 7. Kerrie was assigned to teach two "average" student reading groups, while some students, perhaps one third, moved between teachers for English and social studies. Movement between cores made it more difficult for the teachers to integrate content, a concept basic to the core idea. There were other changes as well, of which two are particularly noteworthy, not only because they represent growing national trends but also because of their effects on Kerrie: She felt threatened by them.

During late fall and without warning, Kerrie received a chart, made of heavy brown paper, that would fit into her roll book and listed all the specific topics she was expected to teach in English and reading. In part this was a reflection of the district's response to the state's effort to produce a core curriculum — yet another national trend. She was thrown into near panic, heightening the persistent tension she felt between the loner's inclination to withdraw and the professional's responsibility to engage issues openly. The expectation relayed was that she should teach each of the objectives and note on the chart the date of instruction — this after three months of the school year had already passed! With the roll book, the chart would be "turned in" to the principal at year's end. Suddenly, the curriculum Kerrie had worked so hard to produce and that she was refining was threatened. What should she do?

Another change came about because the state legislature passed a bill that altered teacher certification requirements. In the past, certification followed graduation from college. In the future, as is becoming increasingly common throughout the United States (Woolever, 1985), a provisional certificate will be given upon graduation, and then, based on a positive outcome of formal quarterly evaluations, a teacher will receive a professional certificate after two years of teaching. In addition, the bill required that beginning teachers be given some kind of support during the two-year probationary period. For Kerrie, this meant that the mentor program that had proven so disappointing during her first year, in part because of lack of funds, would continue into the second, but would be funded. The team leader would continue to be her assigned mentor, but would be paid to conduct quarterly evaluations and to assist Kerrie as needed. The evaluations would be based on a district-adopted form that reflected a very specific vision of what constituted good instruction.

CURRICULUM STANDARDIZATION

As noted in Chapter 6, professionalization of teaching is one of the central ideas driving current educational reform efforts. A key element of professionalism is autonomy. Ironically, at the same time that efforts are being directed toward enhancing teacher autonomy, contradictory efforts are being made to standardize the curriculum for the purposes of accountability, thereby sharply limiting the influence teachers have over the curriculum (Bullough, 1988). The vision of teaching that drives standardization efforts is teaching as instructing, which is perhaps the most commonly held view. Discounting the intimate relationship between the aims and means of education, teachers are free, in this view, to determine the means of instruction but not the aims, which are considered best established by others, perhaps textbook writers, curriculum experts, or citizen committees (Bullough, et al., 1984). As long as instructional aims are somewhat general (leaving teachers a significant degree of interpretative latitude), this view of teaching does not seriously undermine a teacher's feeling of autonomy within the classroom. But when the aims are very specifically stated, perhaps in the form of performance or behavioral objectives, or when the content is stated in minute detail, then the range of teachers' instructional options is severely restricted, sometimes to the point where the means for attainment are prescribed. When this happens, teachers become mere technicians and much of the joy of teaching disappears.

As noted in Chapter 2, for Kerrie, goals and objectives were taken for granted; throughout the year they were implicit in the activities planned. She worried little about them, in part because she was certain she taught what was important for the students to learn. She felt good about her curriculum and the teaching methods she had developed over the first year of teaching, believed the principal supported her program, and looked forward to making improvements in it: "I'm really happy with my curriculum." Moreover, she felt in control of the curriculum: *How much control do you think you have over the curriculum now?* "In my own room?" *Can you do whatever you want?* "Yes, basically, if I can justify it, I think [the principal] would accept it."

It was with shock then that she greeted at the end of the first term the sudden arrival of a sheet containing a long list of specific content objectives that were supposed to be covered over the year: *How does this make you feel?* "Frustrated. Pissed off!" In near panic, Kerrie wondered how she could possibly teach all that was listed in the time remaining: "We were given this and we're supposed to have all these completed by the end of the year . . . we only have three-quarters of the year left to go!" As she reviewed the topics she realized that in some areas there was a poor fit between her curriculum and that contained on the list; something would have to give. The fit between her reading curriculum and the list seemed especially poor: "Three-fourths of this stuff isn't even in the book I use!" Moreover, she had no idea where the list came from or whether it would be reviewed and, if so, for what purposes and by whom: *Where does this come from?* "I don't know. It just appeared on Friday." All she knew was that she was to fill it out by noting the date each topic was taught and then turn it in with the roll book at year's end.

Coverage was not her only concern. Much of the content listed was, she thought, educationally unimportant for seventh graders, undeserving of instructional time. "Someone with a big desk thought some of these up . . . [they're] incredible! Some of it isn't even necessary, I don't think." The list was too specific as well, limiting her range of instructional options: "I don't want them to say you've got to cover these 42 things. I just want them to say, 'The explorers and colonization.' I want general guidelines, I don't want specific [objectives]. Let me cover those general things the way I want to go about it."

Feeling uncertain about how serious the request was and somewhat vulnerable, Kerrie, despite her objections, began planning ways of making her curriculum fit the list. A little stretching here and there would make it possible to date, retroactively, several of the items. Where the stretch would be too much, she would "come up with a way to teach them. I'm going to do the best I can," she said, "I'm attacking it. Maybe I'll take one day a week and cover five things! Then mark off the day. Can you believe it!? I'll do everything I can but if something doesn't get done, all right." She still worried, however: "I've got to talk to other people [on staff] and find out what happens [with this]. I don't know if I'll cover all this stuff. What if I don't? I want to know what happens."

Among the first people she spoke with were the principal and the peer evaluator, who distributed the sheet for the principal. Kerrie wanted to know precisely what the administrators' intentions were. Unfortunately, her questions went unanswered; what she received was a bureaucratic response: The peer evaluator told her the principal wanted the sheet filled out, while the principal said it was a district requirement. In any case, she was given the impression that covering all the listed content was not imperative. In response, she placed on hold any effort to adjust her curriculum. Instead, she viewed the list as filler; she would include an activity designed to accomplish an objective whenever she anticipated having a little instructional time left over from her own curriculum, or when there was a "throw away day," as she called them, a day just before the Christmas break, for instance, when many students would be absent and relatively little teaching could take place: "It's like you do those [activities] when you can't think of what else to do."

Each week, she spent a few minutes, no more than five, she reported, glancing at the list in terms of what the students did during the week and filling in dates. In this way, the sheet gradually would be completed, more or less, while her own curriculum would remain intact. This was Kerrie's way of maintaining control over the curriculum — an essential part of professional autonomy — despite the pressure to standardize. Clearly, the coping strategies she developed during the first year of teaching continued to serve Kerrie into the second. But these too were refined. In Chapter 4 compromise between personal values and institutional requirements as a survival strategy was described. Kerrie's response to accountability pressures reflects a refinement in this strategy: She learned how to engage in minimal compliance, doing just enough to satisfy what was required, but nothing more. It is likely that there is no more frequently used strategy by experienced teachers than this one to soften bureaucratic and administrative demands (Bullough & Gitlin, 1985).

TEACHER MENTORING AND EVALUATION

Teacher mentoring and evaluation are slowly becoming common features of the first year of teaching, although the role of the mentor and the type of evaluation conducted often vary (Galvez-Hjornevik, 1986). Perhaps the most important aspect of the mentor role is that of supporting the beginning teacher (Hegler & Dudley, 1987). As noted, Kerrie received limited support from the team leader during the first year, when mentoring was more a matter of kindness than of school policy. As the year progressed, the team leader, herself a loner, warmed up toward Kerrie. By the second year she and Kerrie were quite friendly, even eating lunch together frequently with a third teacher, which perhaps more than anything else accounted for Kerrie feeling an increased level of support within the school. Kerrie laughingly described her relationship with the team leader during the second year this way: "We all have to have mentors. We call them mentors and mentees. I call [the team leader] my tormentor!" The fact that the team leader was now a paid mentor, or "tormentor," and was quite friendly toward Kerrie did not lead to a significant improvement in the kind and quality of their professional interaction, however. But this was not primarily the team leader's fault; and perhaps there is a lesson to be learned here for educators responsible for designing mentor programs.

Assignment as an Issue

Before considering the specific problems Kerrie and the team leader had with the mentoring program, a general issue should be noted. There is something quite odd about the idea of assigning a mentor, even aside from problems arising from the nature of the relationship established between the team leader and Kerrie over the first year. As Galvez-Hjornevik (1986) puts it:

> Clearly a mentor, in the truest sense of the word, cannot be assigned to a beginning teacher in an induction program. A mentor–protégé pair

connotes a voluntary and deep relationship, not limited to basic direction and encouragement, which more nearly characterizes the responsibilities of a coach. (p. 10)

Kerrie might or might not have chosen the team leader to be her mentor.
But this is not the heart of the matter: She did not have any say at all in
deciding whom she would work with in what could have been her most
significant professional relationship. However, what is a beginning
teacher to do during the first year, before he or she knows and respects
anyone on the faculty? Under these conditions, there seems to be no
reasonable alternative but to assign at least a temporary mentor, taking
the risk, perhaps, of later offense when a permanent one is selected. But
Kerrie was no longer a first-year teacher. She knew a number of faculty
members quite well, and perhaps among these there was an individual
especially well suited to mentoring Kerrie. Reflecting the dominant
view of teacher professionalism discussed in Chapter 6, Kerrie was excluded from participating in the selection process.

Responsibilities of a Mentor

As a mentor, the expectations of the team leader included observing
Kerrie weekly, along with discussing the results of the observations and
conducting a formal evaluation quarterly. To prove that she was carrying out her responsibilities, the team leader was required to keep a log of
her interactions with Kerrie. "My mentor," Kerrie said, "is supposed to
come and watch me once a week but doesn't. She can't, we have the
same preparation [period]." The expectation was that observations
would take place during preparation periods and discussions would
follow. Given the situation, she wondered in frustration, "Obviously,
[the principal] doesn't care. Right?" And so the team leader would
occasionally pop into the class and jot something down so that she could
write it in the log:

> Every once in a while she comes in to see what I'm doing. Like she came
> in one day and I was cutting some blue and white string for when [the
> students] are making books. She said, "Oh, good choice," and went
> back and wrote down in her log: "Kerrie and I discussed the Constitution
> booklets." That's about it. She has to keep a log of the things we discuss,
> but there's nothing for us to do!

The program, Kerrie concluded, was "stupid — I don't need [a men-
tor] on a daily basis to help me. It would have been great last year."

Kerrie mused, "I think that a mentee could benefit . . . from observing the mentor a lot more than being observed. At least in my position, I'd like to watch some teachers teaching. I know what a good and bad teacher looks like."

At this point, which was the middle of the second year, I did something contrary to my understanding with Kerrie, and suggested that she contact the principal to arrange a substitute so that observations could take place. A different tack was taken, however. Following a meeting with the team leader in which Kerrie expressed her concerns, arrangements were made to have the trained peer observer mentioned in Chapter 6 conduct a formal evaluation. But nothing was done to create the conditions necessary for the team leader to carry out her formal mentor responsibilities. Instead, the charade continued.

Evaluation

Kerrie worried about the upcoming evaluations. Nevertheless, she looked forward to the peer teacher evaluation in part because the form would be the same one used later by the principal, who would, based on his evaluation, make a final certification recommendation at the end of the year to the district superintendent. She wanted a practice run to help her prepare for the principal's evaluation. As she reviewed the form, however, she was worried: "There's so much to cover." And she worried about being observed on a bad day: "How could you be the perfect teacher? You couldn't do that every period!" The form itself included 12 items forming a "teacher competence profile": learning objectives, selection and use of instructional materials, instructional activities, and so on. The observer was to assess the quality of performance on a scale of 1 (poor) to 5 (excellent). In addition, there were twelve, two-and-one-half- by three-inch boxes, within which the item was operationally defined and within which comments could be made. For example, under the item, "learning objectives," three statements were given: "Objective or purpose stated to student"; "Responded to student feedback"; and "Checked student understanding."

As Kerrie reviewed the form in anticipation of being evaluated, she interpreted the operational definitions narrowly. Where it said, "Objective or purpose stated to student," Kerrie took that to mean that whenever a formal observation took place, she should begin class by stating an objective in order to gain a high rating. When the day came, she wrote her objective on the board, read it to the students, and, after instruction, read it again. Sure enough, she received a "5" rating along with the comments: "Objective written on board, explained objective." And in the follow-up conference the observer remarked, "Be sure at the end of the period to say [to the students], 'Look at our objective. Did we do this?'" In addition, when the observer entered the room she handed him a typed lesson plan, something experienced teachers rarely write up, and "went right down the list. [I] did everything I said I was going to do." This resulted in receiving the desired check alongside the category, "Thorough preparation of content." In total, of the nine categories rated (for the peer evaluation only nine categories were considered), she received six 5's and three 4's. Kerrie was very pleased, but a bit irritated that she had had to alter her behavior even slightly to fit the list of preferred behaviors in order to gain the desired outcome. Normally, during the second year, she did not write detailed lesson plans, nor did she write her objectives on the board. She would, however, do so whenever she was evaluated in the future. Goffman (1959) describes behavior of this kind as "impression management," a common way of manipulating others to gain desired results.

As Kerrie reflected on this evaluation, she concluded that, as with the two principal evaluations conducted during her first year, she learned little, if anything: *Did you learn anything you didn't know before?* "No. Not really. I'm a decent teacher." It did, however, have the desired effect of preparing her for the principal's evaluation using the new form. For this evaluation she once again wrote out a detailed lesson plan and began class with an objective on the board. But this time she was quite disturbed by the rating, even though it was overwhelmingly positive. Since she followed all the guidelines, she had expected an even more positive evaluation than the first one. Of the twelve categories, she received four 4's and eight 5's. *What had you expected?* "It's not perfect," she said in all seriousness. One of the 4's came because she forgot to restate her objective at the end of the period. Another 4 was accompanied by the remark, "Every time you turn to look to write something on the board the class level of noise rose." This comment was irritating, and she asked the principal what he would do in similar circumstances: "[When I asked him for suggestions] he said, 'Well, let's see now. You could have another student write it on the board. You could use an overhead projector.'" She felt somewhat better, however, by talking with other teachers: "I was really kind of disheartened after I went through it. But then when I talked to other people, they said, 'Oh, that's as good as I get.' We're talking about people who have been teaching ten years compared to my second year here. Then I felt a little bit better."

What disturbed Kerrie most about this and the first evaluation was that she felt she did not gain any insight into how she might improve. After all, if an observer concluded that her instruction was lacking in some way, she thought, and rightly so, the observer had an obligation to be able to articulate what the problem was and how it might be remedied: She wanted to be coached. At the same time, however, she was very disturbed to have received anything less than the highest rating. On one hand, she recognized there were areas within which she needed improvement and she wanted assistance; and on the other, she wanted to be told she was outstanding in every respect and, by implication, not in need of improvement. This dilemma underscores one of the most sensitive issues of teacher evaluation: Teacher evaluation is always more than an assessment of technical skill — which can be improved with coaching — it is also an assessment of the person, and this can be and often is very painful indeed. Receiving all 5's would have been a powerful and welcomed statement from the principal about Kerrie as a person, even though as a teacher she would have realized that such an evaluation would have been faulty. It also underscores a second serious problem: The purposes of teacher evaluation often are confused; a single evaluation system cannot serve both personnel decision-making and teacher improvement goals (Wise et al., 1984). On one hand, it is intended to foster teacher development; on the other, it is intended to rate teacher performance. These are contradictory functions (Gitlin & Bullough, 1987). If development is the goal, and often it sadly is not, then peer evaluation within a context of collegiality ought to be emphasized. It is for this reason that the failure of the mentoring program is most to be lamented. Kerrie's experience with evaluation, with the possible exception of the visit of the peer observer mentioned above, was almost exclusively for the purposes of being rated.

CONCLUSION

On the surface, Kerrie's reaction to the lack of interest in her professional development and to the increasing accountability pressures of the second year may seem a bit surprising in the light of her increasing sense of potency described in the conclusion of Chapter 6. But you will recall that her conception of professionalism was tied to involvement and building community, not to challenging the hierarchical and bureaucratic organization of schooling. She wanted to work within the system to improve it. Moreover, as noted in Chapter 5, when necessary she would compromise some values in order to survive, and clearly, from Kerrie's perspective as a probationary teacher, survival was precisely what was at stake. A positive recommendation from the principal was necessary for certification; thus there were clearly limits to how far she dared to push issues, even in her capacity as association building representative (which raises questions about the wisdom of electing probationary teachers to such important positions). She was torn, not feeling powerful enough to challenge either the system of evaluation or the district's program, yet very unhappy with both.

Kerrie was threatened, insecure. The insecurity she felt, however, was different in some important ways from that of the first year, which was tied closely to problems of teaching such as the unpredictability of the students and the uncertainty of lesson outcomes. During the second year, however, she was confident that she was a good teacher; this was not an issue. Indeed, her evaluations concluded that she was an "excellent" teacher. And yet, judgments of her teaching competence would be made based on compliance with policies and externally established standards of behavior. If she did not comply, or at least appear to be in compliance, she feared a negative evaluation and a quick end to her dream of being a teacher. Under these pressures minimal compliance presents itself as an appealing strategy; after all, she was a probationary teacher, however competent she was.

Feeling powerless, the reaction of teachers to evaluation and accountability pressures of this kind typically is to withdraw and "cover your ass" (CYA). Kerrie was no different. Withdrawal, which facilitates minimal compliance, is a survival strategy that is very much a part of the culture of teaching generally, as it was within Rocky Mountain Junior High School specifically. This was noted in Chapter 3 when Kerrie hesitated to seek assistance and addressed her problems alone. Much has been written about the culture of teaching that has developed in response to working conditions like those noted in Chapter 6. It is presentist, concerned only with the here and now; conservative (teachers resist reform and take few risks); and individualistic (teachers tend to go it alone) (Bullough, 1987). Given this culture, and the values that infuse it, there is considerable subtle pressure to withdraw; withdrawal appears commonsensical. Through withdrawal teachers try to maintain their personal values, while minimally satisfying institutional demands and expectations. Through withdrawal teachers feel a kind of autonomy, although at the cost of accepting isolation. And so, by withdrawing, Kerrie responded in a manner common to teachers; as an individual she adopted a conservative strategy of minimal compliance to institutional requirements. But given the increasing influence of teacher evaluation and accountability, one must ask: Where is a secure place within which to withdraw? And, what good comes from withdrawing in order to CYA through minimal compliance?

Even as Kerrie withdrew she knew, based on her experience of the first year, that withdrawal was but a temporary and partial solution to the problem of meeting administrator expectations while preserving her curriculum and the values on which it rested, and no solution at all to her dissatisfaction with the teacher mentoring and evaluation programs. Yet again, an internal tug of war began to take place between the loner and the beginning-teacher professional. Her classroom was certainly not a very secure place, as she well knew; after all, the physical arrangement made observation easy. But more important, mentoring and teacher evaluation would continue to be means by which those in positions of authority could at will breach the classroom walls (which clearly was what they were intended to accomplish, among other aims). With this knowledge, the loner side seemed to stumble: Kerrie knew that power would come only through informed involvement with other teachers sharing her concerns. She would have to reach outside of herself, although temporarily she closed in. Ultimately she would have to engage other teachers, even if she, as a probationary teacher, was not yet in a position to challenge administrative decisions. In the quest to come to terms with accountability and evaluation issues, a vital, teacher-controlled mentoring program that emphasized teacher support and development while minimizing rating and ranking would have been very helpful to her. Unfortunately, such a program did not exist for Kerrie. Perhaps in the future she and other teachers who share her concerns will be able to help create one, for by law there will be a mentoring program, for good or ill. In the meantime, Kerrie will anxiously await final certification and the security that comes with being tenured.

QUESTIONS FOR CONSIDERATION

1. What would you have done in Kerrie's place when suddenly presented with a list of specific items to be taught? Did she behave responsibly? Professionally? Sensibly?
2. Have you ever effectively used impression management to obtain a favorable evaluation from a "superior"? Is this a desirable strategy to use, since at least on the surface it appears to be a form of planned deception? Given Kerrie's situation, what would you have done? What alternatives are there?
3. Given that one of the characteristics of a profession is that members "police" other members, why do teachers frequently object to being rated by peers? Do you see any benefit to peer ratings? What kinds of information and help would you most like to have from a mentor?

4. Does Kerrie's reaction to the principal's evaluation seem reasonable? Would you have been disappointed, as she was? Why or why not?
5. Do you agree with the author's assessment that withdrawal is no solution to Kerrie's problems? If so, why is withdrawal so tempting to teachers?

ACTIVITIES

1. If your state is one of the many that have recently passed legislation leading to the establishment of teacher mentor programs, obtain a copy of the law. Read it, paying particular attention to the rights and responsibilities of the mentor and the beginning teacher. What is the bill's intention: rating or teacher development (or are these purposes confused?)? Critique it in the light of what you believe you will most need to help make your first year or two of teaching successful and enjoyable.
2. The culture of teaching is characterized in this chapter as being conservative, presentist, and individualistic. Ask a teacher you respect whether he or she shares this view. If so, ask what its effects are on the quality of the teacher's work life. And, if you dare, ask what the person is doing to alter the situation. If not, ask the teacher what makes the culture of his or her school different? Who or what is it that makes the difference?

Concluding Remarks

By the end of her first year of teaching, Kerrie was well into the mastery stage of teaching. Her second year, in many ways a refinement of the first, brought with it a growing sense of competence and power, although, as noted in Chapter 8, she remained vulnerable to outside influences. Among the changes that took place, several bear repetition: Through the development of an array of skills and understandings, management and discipline slipped as primary concerns, to be replaced by student learning and motivation. This change prompted another: As the year progressed, Kerrie actually seemed to enjoy the students more. Part of her success came because she established and consistently reinforced a set of reasonable standards for academic and behavioral performance. She became "stricter," as she said she would, and yet maintained a sense of humor, which played a pivotal role in her generally successful quest to establish a "fun" classroom. Having developed a solid understanding of the students, when planning she only occasionally thought of her own children and their likes and dislikes and she thought little if at all about her own experience as a teen-ager, as she had formerly done. Indeed, by the second year she seemed to know her students before actually meeting them. Relationships with other teachers on the faculty improved immensely, especially with the team leader, who included Kerrie among a small group of confidants. She developed an intimate, although far from complete, knowledge of how the school worked, and with this knowledge she became increasingly sophisticated at manipulating the institution to help ease the problem of negotiating a satisfying place within it. Moreover, through her election as association building representative, she began establishing herself as a key player within the school. Home and work remained separate, but the boundary was weakened because of the decision to do more grading of the quality of student work and to make a more concerted effort to inform parents. And, in general, she became more reflective about practice.

These are some of the changes that took place; happily some things remained the same. Kerrie continued in the resolve to be an outstanding teacher and to this end she engaged in continuous teacher education through inservice course work. Although battered at times, her enthusiasm for teaching remained intact. She worked hard from the beginning of the first year onward, although not always efficiently; efficiency came with experience. She maintained her dedication to producing a varied curriculum, despite student resistance to unusual activities. And, Kerrie kept laughing.

Appendix A
A Note on Method

Much has been written lately on what is or ought to be the attitude taken by a researcher toward his or her subject. There is no consensus. Even among researchers who support the value of observational studies there are sharp disagreements. Some researchers argue that the only reasonable approach is one of strict neutrality. No matter what happens in a classroom, the aim of the researcher is to objectively and dispassionately record events in some fashion for later analysis. The teacher is literally an object being studied. Others argue that researchers inevitably influence the phenomena they study; the researcher's obligation is to be as clear as is possible about the nature of that influence so that caution will be taken whenever the temptation arises to generalize from the data.

Oddly, many of the debates over methodology focus almost entirely on the influence of the researcher on the data, while comparatively little attention is given to the ethical dimension of conducting research: What is the researcher's obligation to the persons being studied? Is it reasonable and ethically responsible, for example, to withhold information that could, in the hands of the teacher being observed, prevent serious difficulty for either the teacher or the students being taught? And, is it morally responsible to withhold the conclusions reached or to present them without making provision for meeting with those observed to discuss the results so that whatever educational potential they possess might be extracted?

These are tough issues, but I shall try to address them, however briefly. I believe it is not morally responsible to withhold critical information, and as a result I have had a degree of influence on this study that may be grounds for a measure of criticism. From time to time in my interviews with Kerrie I shared insights that seemed important to share, as when I suggested she make arrangements with the team leader for a substitute so observations could take place. When Kerrie asked questions, I responded, although throughout our time together she understood that my role was emphatically not to tell her what to do. Indeed, she was quite clear about this: Had I attempted to function in a teacher role, she would have withdrawn from the project. In addition, beginning about March of the first year, I shared, and we discussed, my written interpretations of the events that transpired. This was done not only to confirm the accuracy of my understanding, which is fundamental, but also to provide her with an opportunity to critique my work and to use it as a source of feedback if she wished to do so.

During critique sessions and in three separate formal interviews we discussed our relationship and the nature of my influence. Perhaps the best way to describe this is to let Kerrie speak for herself. These quotes come from an interview conducted during May of the first year.

Do you do anything differently when I am here? I don't think I ever have, really. *There is a lot of research on impression management, where . . .* the principal comes down and you give the model lesson. *Yes, you've done that for him.* [I've been] a little more inventive, maybe. But I haven't especially changed what I was doing in the first place. *So, you don't do things differently [when I'm here]?* No, I do look ahead and think, "Oh, look what I'm going to be doing. Bob is here. He is going to see this!" The thing is, you are here often enough that you see the day-to-day things. I couldn't fix up every week. You pretty much see it like it is, I would say. The only changes you make are idea changes in my mind about how I see things. *What do you mean by that?* I've just become more critical. Sometimes I just kind of stop and think, now, what would Bob think of this? It's not even classroom things; sometimes it is what other teachers are saying or things . . . that would happen in a faculty meeting. *Why would I have any influence over your doing that?* You always come [to our interviews] with questions to ask that I don't really even think about. . . .

Do you think the students behave differently [because I'm in the classroom]? I don't think so. As a matter of fact, it's shocking to me that they don't behave differently. *Why is that?* It just seems to me if there was another adult watching . . . (pause). They do ask me all the time, "Why is that guy here?" I have told them 100 times, but it's like they just don't get it. I don't think it phases them in the least [to have you here]. They just go on. . . .

Do you think that our conversations have had any effect on how you have developed professionally? I think [so,] absolutely. [But] it's really hard to put a finger on it (pause). OK, this is what I want to say. It gives me . . . assurance. I'm pretty assured already, but there's just more of it. *How would you account for that?* Just being able to talk. The questions you ask me make me really think. Sometimes I think about them, all week long. It really has that effect. It has made a change weekly. We've talked about these things on a weekly basis. . . .

Have you been disappointed [in me]? No. [Our relationship is] pretty much just what I thought [it would be]. *At times I wanted to be dealing with some of these kids. I felt a constant tension but, I realized I couldn't do that.* That [action would have spoiled] the whole thing. If I knew you were going to say "why don't you do that?" it would just, it would spoil it. . . .

So, your perception of me is that I am nonjudgmental? Yes, very much so. It makes me really comfortable having you here because if I knew someone was going to be really critiquing me, that just wouldn't work. I have always felt really good because I feel [that] if I want to know something, you'll tell me.

According to Kerrie, I have helped her feel more self-assured and influenced her to be more critically minded about her work: "Every time I talk to you . . . it's just a catalyst because it makes me think about what I'm doing. It's not necessarily you, it's me thinking more about me." I am pleased with both outcomes, although they were unintended. Apparently, the hours spent talking about her work and the reasons underlying certain observed actions have subtly affected how she understands herself and teaching. What I have not done is alter how either she or the students have behaved in any fundamental way nor, more important, have I had any influence over the kinds of problems she faced during her first year of teaching, which were, generally speaking, quite typical.

Appendix B

Comments on Teacher Education

Beginning teachers frequently complain bitterly about the inadequacy of their teacher preparation programs. Kerrie, too, had some complaints. In Chapter 4, mention was made of her dissatisfaction with the emphasis placed on grading, for example. But initially her teacher education seemed more irrelevant to her performance in the classroom than inadequate. She enjoyed the classes she took and appreciated the support she received: "[The program is] special . . . everyone [had] the same goals. [The professors] wanted to help us, and we wanted to be helped." And she claimed to have learned a great deal, but during the first several weeks of teaching there seemed to be little evidence of it. As one of her instructors, I found this troubling, to say the least. In this appendix we briefly explore the place of teacher education in Kerrie's movement toward the mastery stage of teaching.

LIMITED IMPACT

As noted in Chapter 3, with respect to planning, little seemed to have transferred from Kerrie's teacher education to her actual classroom practice: She did not plan as taught, nor did she plan in advance for management. On the surface, the conclusion that seems to follow is that teacher education was a waste of time: Certainly, if ideas as basic as these did not transfer, then perhaps nothing of worth was learned. We shall briefly consider each problem.

Systematic Planning

For Kerrie, thinking about goals and objectives was a low priority, without some kind of external impetus to do so. She did not think carefully about what she wanted from the students, which contributed, early in the first year, to her occasional sense of being adrift. When questioned in interviews about her goals and objectives early in the first year, they were vague and uncertain, even though she admitted the desirability of their becoming more clear. Her lack of attention to goals and objectives was not, however, exceptional. She did not see other teachers attending to them, which justified the omission, and perhaps inadvertently encouraged production of the list handed down from the district offices in the late fall of her second year. Moreover, she was under a great deal of pressure to perform and had little time to spend reflecting on goals. Clearly, under the intense and immediate demands of day-to-day teaching—one source of the presentism mentioned in Chapter 8—beginning teachers are frequently too busy running to know precisely where they are going; the aim is just to keep moving. And so, on the surface at least, the experience of teaching in Rocky Mountain Junior High School appeared to wash out whatever she might have gained from the study of planning in her teacher education program. And yet this may be too hasty a conclusion.

As McCutcheon (1982) noted a few years ago, teacher planning is primarily a mental activity, a form of problem solving. Initially there was a logic evident in Kerrie's planning: Her thinking moved from a concern with activities to time, with purposes taken for granted. As the year progressed, her thinking changed, however: Activities were seen in the light of purposes and student ability and interests, and in relationship to time constraints. When making a planning decision, her thoughts would race among these elements. With this change, which came near the end of the survival stage, insights gained from her teacher education course work surfaced. Referring to one set of courses in particular, she commented:

[The professor] always said take the students from where they are to where you want them to go. She was always very questioning about what your [purposes] were [but she didn't just ask] what's your objective. It was more than that: What is the student thinking, where is he or she? What do you want [them] to be doing? Whenever I have to prepare a lesson, I'm thinking about how to be creative [with it]; she always [emphasized] creative things. I go back to those [things she taught]. Sometimes I even go back and thumb through lessons that [the students in her classes] did [and shared] with each other. That helps a lot.

These ideas seemed to return only after the first stormy months of teaching had passed and Kerrie began to feel a measure of control over her classes and her work life. To that point, she had sometimes reacted and responded to the environment as though almost under siege. With a little breathing space came the inclination to be more self-critical and reflective, and in the process she rediscovered her teacher education, or at least a portion of it.

Planning for Discipline and Management

As noted at the beginning of Chapter 3, Kerrie's explanation of her failure to plan adequately for management was that she simply did not think it necessary, despite the emphasis placed on it in her teacher education program. In this respect, Kerrie is likely quite unusual since discipline and management tend to be the principal concerns of student teachers. Nevertheless, her experience underscores two common problems: Student teaching and the first year of teaching are remarkably different experiences; and often the messages given during university course work are countered by field experience. In Kerrie's student teaching, planning for management obviously was not required, since she entered a classroom already reasonably well routinized, perhaps rule bound, where student passivity was much more of a problem than acting out. While not having to plan for management freed her to plan the curriculum, it also encouraged the development of a lopsided view of planning: Discipline and management will fall almost automatically into place if only there is good curriculum planning. Clearly, this is not the case, as has been shown.

When Kerrie realized that planning for discipline and management was necessary, some of the lessons of teacher education returned, albeit slowly. The importance of paying close attention to transitions and to pacing were among the lessons she recalled. Another was the value of consistency: "You told us consistency was the key. It is the truth, it is the gospel." In a related vein, when dealing with differences in ability, she tapped information presented in two of her preparation courses: "I think it was in our [classes together] that we talked about all the different methods of learning. So, I'm trying to use all of those." Some odd ideas cropped up as well. For example, in one class she was told to never touch students: "Right now do you know what this child needs? A hug, but I can't give it to [him]. *Why?* Because that is what [a professor] told us, never to touch our students."

Apparently, teacher education was not unimportant to Kerrie's development, but it certainly did not have the power that any of her instructors, myself included, wanted. This weakness needs to be accounted for. Doing so reveals an extremely important set of problems that needs to be attended to by teacher educators and beginning teachers: the ease with which beginning teachers are seduced by the myth of familiarity, and the dangers of being seduced into incompetence by common sense.

TEACHER BIOGRAPHY AND COMMON SENSE

Part of the explanation of the limited influence of teacher education has been touched on already. The intensity of the demands placed on beginning teachers and the struggle merely to survive make it difficult to put into place some of the ideas presented during teacher education. And one wonders: How well can the lessons of teacher education be learned, even if they are good ones, given the paucity of hours dedicated to teacher education in most college and university programs? Teaching is infinitely more complex than the practice of law, yet law school programs typically are three years in length while teacher education programs often are no more than one year long! The Holmes Group is correct: If teacher education is to have significant influence on students, then it must be of longer duration and greater intensity than is currently the practice (Holmes Group, 1986). Moreover, some ideas are not applied because they do not seem to fit the context or they seem unimportant; for example, including formal statements of goals and objectives in planning. Part of the difficulty is that the schools and teacher education programs are based upon different sets of values; sometimes they actually send contradictory messages to the beginning teacher about what is appropriate practice. Each of these problems requires the careful attention of teacher educators.

Additional reasons for the limited influence of teacher education quickly come to mind, but for beginning teachers, one in particular deserves attention, in part because of how powerful it is and in part because it is so often ignored. Recent research suggests that prospective teachers, like Kerrie, frequently bring with them into their teacher education programs a very strong sense of self as teacher (Crow, 1987). This identity, or self-image, which formed from years of observing teaching as a student and from other biographical influences such as Kerrie's experience as a mother, is the source of teacher common sense, the "socialized logic" noted in the conclusion of Chapter 3 (Crow, 1987).

The beginning teacher's identity as a teacher and the common sense that flows from it form a fine interpretive lens or filter through which the teacher views his or her preparation. Ideas, concepts, and even skills that do not fit the beginning teacher's self-image, which is accepted as right and proper, and are not backed up with sufficient power to prompt internalization through practice or through experiences that demonstrate conclusively their value, are screened out. On the other hand, ideas that confirm a vision of self as teacher are highlighted and seen as credible. In part this selective process is possible because virtually everyone takes teaching and what teachers do for granted, having spent innumerable hours in classrooms. (Excluding college, "the new teacher has logged somewhere between sixteen and eighteen thousand hours in classrooms before taking over a class" [Ryan, 1986, p. 17].) Beginning teachers are often seduced into a false security by the familiarity of teaching, only later to discover that not all is as it seems. They are strangers in a familiar land (Ryan, 1986).

Very early in Kerrie's first year of teaching, she reflected the view that those who emerged from teacher education programs as good teachers entered that way: "The best teachers," she said, "are the ones who are [already] the best teachers." What teacher education could provide were some of the "tricks of the trade," she said. In addition, through "positive critiques" it could help the novice sharpen teaching skills that were already possessed and thereby improve "self-confidence." For her, teacher education confirmed her intuition and common sense and in this there was value, "tons" of it: There was value in being given "a lot of commonsense things [even though] I'd think, 'that's stupid, anyone with a brain would think of that.'" The value came in the confirmation of self. For example, on one occasion in the middle of September of the first year, she remarked that giving positive feedback following student responses was "the natural thing to do." She then made reference to the time during her teacher education when the topic was discussed following the reading of selected research in the area. She did not remember the research, which included discussion of the limitations on the effectiveness of positive feedback as a means for enhancing the learning of some types of students, nor on how teachers tend to use it differentially and unequally:

I don't know, I just [do] it. [Before entering the teacher education program] I already knew [to do] it. I don't think about it at all. It's not something I ever tried to develop. I remember we talked about it, but it just seemed like the natural thing to do. *Natural?* Like, why should someone have to tell you that? That's dumb. That's normal. What else would you say?

Nonetheless, it pleased her to know she was presumably doing the right thing.

As noted, reliance on common sense, what was "natural," proved to be a source of some of Kerrie's most serious problems, even though, generally speaking, it served her reasonably well. One problem was quite surprising: Her tendency to discount information that did not quite fit her self-image in a few instances led to a discounting of the sources of that knowledge, with unhappy results. An example comes from the time when Kerrie was struggling to produce a satisfying grading system. As noted, she criticized her teacher education program for failing to adequately emphasize grading practices. In an interview she commented on the text used in the course that addressed grading: "I haven't used [the text]. It was useful when we were learning about it; I thought it had a good section in there." This said, she did not refer to the book, even though it may very well have helped her resolve some of the problems then troubling her. Instead, she struggled through the problems on her own, relying on her own experiences, primarily those as a student, for answers.

As the year progressed, Kerrie's common sense became less common. Some of her most cherished beliefs were challenged and adjustments were made as she came to terms with the teaching role presented to her by Rocky Mountain Junior High School. She had to unlearn, as well as learn, to become a competent teacher. Generally speaking, the impact of her teacher education program in this process was modest, but not unimportant.

CONTINUOUS TEACHER EDUCATION

Kerrie seemed to separate clearly her university teacher education from the inservice education available through the school district. By the second year, the value of the former was that it provided a good foundation for continuing her professional education. Indeed, at the beginning of her second year, she spoke of her university teacher education almost as though it was a kind of general education for teaching, of enduring but unspecified importance, there when needed as a source of ideas and understandings:

> What if you hadn't done any university teacher education? So, what difference would it make? A lot. I couldn't teach without all of that. Why not? Gosh! That's a hard question. My word! (pause) It matures you . . . it . . . changes the person you are, . . . it makes you a different person . . . you have a different outlook.

But it was more than just a general education; it was a source of ideas that could be tapped:

> When it comes to . . . the [study of] teaching itself, I learned lots of techniques that I think [back on]. You also benefit from hearing [suggestions] about how to do [mundane things] like . . . how to have [outside guests] come into your classroom. I can still recall little things that [some professors] said. Watching [other students] teach a lesson and being able to see what was wrong with it [was helpful]. [It helped me to] be critical of what I do in order to change it [which is] one of the most important aspects of [my education].

In contrast, inservice courses were imminently and immediately practical: They took place while she was teaching, dealt with topics and issues of immediate concern, and were taught by teachers. Both were valuable, but in different ways, and they connected as part of her experience.

While it is unfortunate that such clear distinctions should exist between university and school-based inservice programs—and these differences were not just in Kerrie's mind—what is important is that she concluded her university course work apparently believing that part of being a teacher was to engage in continuous professional education—that is what professionals do. In retrospect, she realized her university course work could not possibly have included everything necessary to being a fully competent teacher within a specific context like Rocky Mountain Junior High School, which undoubtedly accounted for some of her favorable attitude toward teacher education. Throughout the first year Kerrie constantly took inservice courses to either improve her content area background (courses related specifically to the courses she was teaching) or to gain useful instructional ideas. To draw on the law analogy again, her image seemed to be that teachers practice teaching as lawyers practice law. This is an extremely important insight, one essential to professionalism, to be sure, but perhaps even more fundamental to staying alive intellectually and emotionally as a teacher.

A PERSONAL NOTE TO TEACHER EDUCATORS

First-Year Teacher was written to and for beginning teachers, but a word to teacher educators needs to be said. The year-and-a-half spent in Kerrie's classroom, along with other ongoing projects, have caused me to engage in some rather difficult soul-searching. While I was a bit relieved to know that my part in Kerrie's teacher education had some influence on her performance during the first year of teaching, I am far from pleased with how modest it was. In the light of this discovery I have reconsidered much of what I did in the past and have made some changes in content, among other things. But, of even greater importance, I have become more dedicated to working to bring about the reform of teacher education generally.

Clearly, the reform of teacher education is but one part of a much larger agenda now being addressed by numerous groups throughout the nation, including the Holmes Group and the Carnegie Forum. The task is nothing short of the reformation of American education. It is self-evident: Improved and powerful teacher education is dependent on improved practicum sites (schools) and improved college and university programs in the disciplines and in general education. As I conclude this book, however, I must set aside these important concerns and focus on more modest aims.

Structurally, teacher education must extend into the first years of teaching. In this regard the momentum building behind the development of mentor programs is encouraging. What is discouraging is that so few mentor programs appear to actively involve college and university personnel and that so many are concerned with making personnel decisions rather than nurturing beginning teachers. It is also a bit discouraging to note that so many mentor programs, like Kerrie's, ignore the importance to teacher development of adjustments in the role and responsibilities of the beginning teacher. Beginning teachers should have fewer preparations to do than experienced, expert teachers, and they should not be assigned to the most difficult groups of students, as was Kerrie during her first year. Again, drawing on the lawyer analogy, a rookie lawyer is not assigned a complex murder case for his or her first assignment! Beginning teachers should be assigned a dedicated, and paid, mentor — an expert teacher who can articulate the grounds of his or her expertise — who is given released time to work with the novice, who is responsible for assisting in professional development and for being an advocate or "sponsor" (Anderson & Shannon, 1988), but not for conducting formal performance evaluations used for either licensure or employment decisions. Though frequently confused (Darling-Hammond & Berry, 1988) these functions, which should be placed in the hands of teachers as professionals, must be separated, as they are by law in California (Shulman & Colbert, 1987). If, for some unfortunate reason, performance evaluation is the responsibility of the mentor, then the novice should also evaluate the mentor's performance as a mentor; mentors should have a stake in the beginner's success or failure. I said that beginning teachers should be "assigned" a mentor. This assignment might be a very short one; during the first few weeks of teaching the beginner ought to be able to observe other teachers, perhaps from a short list, seeking to identify a mentor; for the mentor, being chosen should not only bring an increase in pay, it should also be a recognized professional honor.

Beginning teachers desperately need to talk, but too often they do not have anyone to talk to; that is, anyone who knows something about teaching, has seen them teach, and is not in a formal evaluative position. Kerrie's team members might have served this function for her, but they did not. Provision should be made for linking beginning teachers together into groups formed explicitly for support and for the study of practice. Obviously, the study of practice should include participation in peer observations (which was something Kerrie badly wanted to be involved in). Similarly, pre-service teacher education should be organized, as was Kerrie's, around a cohort ideal which, when effectively implemented, can serve as a model professional community.

For teacher educators thinking through course content, careful attention needs to be given to their students' values developed over many years of school attendance, among other sources. We ought to recognize and honor the idiosyncratic nature of teaching, not flee from it. Without question, these values and the teacher identity that carries them play a central role in the socialization process and can be ignored only at the cost of a good education (Zeichner, 1986). Let me give an example, from my work with a group of students, of one attempt to respond to student values that arose because of insights gained from this study: Given the realities of teaching, and the nature of planning, it may not be sensible to expect to find beginning teachers systematically producing detailed written plans complete with goal statements. But this does not mean that it does not make sense to study planning; rather it suggests that planning be approached as a form of problem solving that necessitates attention to a wide range of variables that affect student learning and teacher security and satisfaction. Ultimately, the point of studying planning is to become a better planner, and a better problem solver, and in this process it makes a great deal of sense to study and experiment with various formal models of planning. The student should do this with an eye toward identifying and improving his or her own approach, not emulating someone else's idea of good planning. In this light, I am now having my students formulate, study, and critique their own and their classmates' approaches to planning as a form of problem solving.

Other changes in content might also be desirable. The current push to increase the amount of time spent in schools is one such change evident in many of the programs of teacher education being hailed as innovative (The NETWORK, 1987). But a strong word of caution is in order: More field experience may actually be miseducative unless it is carefully articulated with university or college work and brings the student into contact with the best educational practices. Otherwise, field work may actually do more harm than good (think of the influence of Kerrie's student teaching on her view of discipline and management, for instance). In a related vein, given that reform is going to take a good long while, perhaps the content of teacher education should be expanded to include instruction in the skills necessary for institutional survival, skills like those Kerrie developed that helped her negotiate a reasonably satisfying role. Many of our better students quit teaching because of frustrating work conditions, not for reasons associated with teaching and working with young people. But here too, a warning is in order: Such skills should be taught within the wider context of the development of the attitudes, skills, and concepts associated with the creation of a professional community of critical discourse. Fundamentally, teacher education programs ought to reflect a dedication to and participation within such a community, not a dedication to coping per se, or to the kind of self-righteous faultfinding that characterizes so many teacher education courses.

As I have said before, for good or ill the struggle through the first year of teaching creates a pattern of behavior and understanding that is played out in subsequent years. It is at this time more than any other that teachers need to be helped to think through their values in the light of the demands of the disciplines of knowledge, the characteristics of young people, the social responsibilities of schooling, and the pressures of institutional life. It is only by helping them to do so that the view now prevalent — that teaching is synonymous with instructing and managing classes, and little concerned with establishing the aims of education — can be challenged. This is essential to education reform. Teaching is more than technique. It is an art, a moral craft, and a science. Teacher education programs that help students to understand this have a vital role to play in addressing the general problem of education renewal facing America. Those that do not, stand as obstacles to teacher professionalization and are part of the problem.

Appendix C

Advice on Selecting a School and Surviving the Year

Changing a work context to make it more conducive to professional development is very difficult. For teachers who have yet to assume their first positions, the sensible route is to do everything possible to obtain employment within the best available work context. A brief discussion of what to look for when choosing a school follows. Then a few suggestions will be presented that may help make your first year of teaching go more smoothly.

ASSESSING A SCHOOL

At first glance it may seem a little odd to speak about choosing a work context, since memories of recent and serious teacher oversupply and unemployment linger. But, generally speaking, those times are now past. We are facing serious teacher shortages in many content areas and in many locations in the country. Many beginning teachers have a choice of jobs; Kerrie, for example, had three offers.

When selecting a school, simple things may be extremely important, as we shall see. But first, when reviewing the list that follows, it is important to recognize up front that any one item may be of little consequence. It is when factors are considered together that there is reason for either concern or delight. Moreover, no setting is likely to be perfectly good or perfectly bad. Some weighing of evidence will be necessary when making a decision. Finally, it should be noted that depending on the timing of an offer, some of the suggestions that follow may be impossible to implement; for example, if an offer comes after school has closed for the year. In any case, given the importance of the decision, it is worth taking time to think it over and do some checking.

1. Ask the principal why the job you are being offered is open. Did it become available because a first-year teacher quit, or because someone retired? Ask what kind of turnover rate there is in the building. A generally stable faculty is a good sign.
2. When walking into a building notice whether or not it is clean. A dirty building suggests lack of pride, and lack of pride may indicate serious problems within the school. Watch out!
3. Notice if the building seems orderly. Are students wandering the hallways when classes are in session? When the bell rings, do students continue to talk and only at their convenience make their way to class? Or, when the bell rings, is there a rush to be on time? The latter action suggests the students take school seriously, which is a good sign for those charged with teaching; student complacency is very difficult to overcome.
4. Notice if the teachers' doors are open or shut when class is in session. There are many reasons for doors to be closed (a noisy ventilation system, for example), but some of these reasons have to do with teachers being in hiding. Where isolation is the norm, professional development suffers.
5. Wander the hallways as school ends to see how long the teachers stay in their rooms past the final bell. If teachers flee the building en masse, they may be sending a message that they do not like being there.
6. Talk to a few teachers randomly to find out if they feel supported by the administration and whether or not the administration recognizes teacher and student performance. Ask, for example, who the principal generally backs when there is a disagreement between a parent and a teacher. Ask if the administration awards letters to students for academic excellence or in other ways lets the students know that they are in school to learn. If so, it is a good sign.
7. Visit the faculty lunchroom at lunch time. Is it a lively, friendly place? If so, it is a good sign. If not, ask where the teachers eat. If they eat in their rooms in clusters of two or three, then establishing professional relationships will likely be very difficult.
8. Ask a couple of teachers to describe school governance and what part teachers play in decision making. Ask them personally how they are involved. Look for committees that deal with genuine issues and have significant teacher representation on them. Lack of such committees may mean teachers' opinions are not respected.
9. Visit a faculty meeting. Are the teachers and administrators friendly toward one another? Are issues openly and honestly discussed? What does it feel like to be there?

10. Locate a new teacher in the building and ask if there is a mentor program and if so what he or she has gained from it. In particular ask what the purposes of the program are: ranking or teacher development? And ask what kind of support you might expect as a first-year teacher.

11. Review a copy of the district's teacher contract to find out precisely what the formal teacher role and responsibilities are. In particular review carefully that portion of the document that addresses due process. Find out what the boundaries of appropriate behavior are, for in them resides a view of teacher professionalism that may or may not be conducive to your growth.

12. Ask someone in the department or area within which you will be teaching whether or not they have adequate materials with which to teach. Lack of materials may indicate lack of support.

SURVIVING THE FIRST YEAR

Once you accept a position, there are a few bits of advice that may help you survive the first year. The following list is composed of items drawn from Ryan (1986), from Kerrie's experience, and from my own work with teachers.

1. *"Before you begin the first year of teaching, decide to teach a second* [italics in original]. The first year of teaching is a unique situation. There is so much that is new and so much to learn that it is foolish to make judgments based on only one year's experience" (Ryan, 1986, p. 31).

2. *If you are not assigned one, find a mentor.* "Find an experienced, older teacher who is willing to act as a guide and confidant through the first year" (Ryan, 1986, p. 33).

3. *Make certain you know and understand school policies and regulations, especially respecting discipline and management.* Knowing beforehand precisely where you stand and what you can and cannot do will help you deal appropriately when surprising situations arise, as they inevitably will.

4. *Plan carefully and get organized.* "One of the great surprises of the first year is the amount of paperwork and the number of details that are part of the teacher's life" (Ryan, 1986, p. 32). If you are not well prepared and organized, it is easy to be smothered by the demands of teaching.

5. *Get to know your students, but do not expect to make friends in the process.* The quicker you get to know your students well, the easier

it will be to plan an appropriate curriculum for them and to identify teaching strategies likely to lead to learning. But in the process, you want respect from them, not love, although love may come.

6. *Reach out and engage other faculty members; become involved.* Isolation is a real threat not only to survival but to the development of professionalism. Eat lunch with other teachers. Volunteer to be a member (not a chair) of a few carefully selected committees that will help you build relationships. Join the association. Go to faculty parties.

7. *"Pay your body its dues.* Stress is a fact of life in the first year. The demands of time and energy can lead to a loss of sleep, poor eating habits, and little real exercise. Together they can lead directly to health problems: lingering colds, anxiety, and depression. It is especially important that the new teacher get adequate rest, eat nutritious meals, and exercise regularly. These are not luxuries to be sacrificed to the demands of the job; they are necessities of the job" (Ryan, 1986, p. 33).

8. *Befriend the secretary and maintenance person.* Secretaries and maintenance people can make life easy or hard for the beginning teacher. They know how to get things done, where to obtain materials, and often whom to go for to get decent help when it is needed.

9. *"Come to terms with your authority.* Few young people have had much experience as an authority figure. They would much rather have things run smoothly without them having to tell students what to do or correct their behavior. But as a teacher you have authority and you are in charge. Also, your colleagues, your administrators, your parents, and especially your students all want you to exercise your authority responsibly. The alternative is failure and chaos" (Ryan, 1986, p. 33).

10. *Laugh and forgive yourself.* You are bound to make mistakes, learn from them, laugh at them, and forgive yourself; tomorrow is another day!

11. *Remember what goes well.* You will have both good and bad days. Sometimes it is difficult to remember the good days. Enjoy your successes and learn from them, as you do from your mistakes.

References

Anderson, E. M. & Shannon, A. L. (1988). Toward a conceptualization of mentoring. *Journal of Teacher Education, 39*(1), 38–42.

Apple, M. (1979). *Ideology and curriculum*. Boston: Routledge & Kegan Paul.

Berliner, D. C. (1986). In pursuit of the expert pedagogue. *Educational Researcher, 15*(7), 1–23.

Brophy, J. & Kher, N. (1986). Teacher socialization as a mechanism for developing student motivation to learn. In R. Feldman (Ed.), *Social psychology applied to education* (pp. 257–88). Cambridge: Cambridge University Press.

Bullough, R. V. Jr. (1987). Accommodation and tension: Teachers, teacher role, and the culture of teaching. In J. Smyth (Ed.), *Educating teachers: Changing the nature of pedagogical knowledge* (pp. 83–94). London: The Falmer Press.

Bullough, R. V. Jr. (1988). *The forgotten dream of American public education*. Ames, Iowa: Iowa State University Press.

Bullough, R. V. Jr. & Gitlin, A. (1985). Beyond control: Rethinking teacher resistance. *Education and Society, 3*(1), 65–73.

Bullough, R. V. Jr. & Gitlin, A. (1986). Limits of teacher autonomy: Decision-making, ideology and reproduction of role. *New Education, 6*(1), 25–34.

Bullough, R. V. Jr., Goldstein, S. L., & Holt, L. (1984). *Human interests in the curriculum: Teaching and learning in a technological society*. New York: Teachers College Press, Chapter 2.

Canter, L. (1977). *Assertive discipline: A take-charge approach for today's educator*. Los Angeles, California: Canter & Associates, Inc.

Clark, C. M. & Peterson, P. L. (1986). Teachers' thought processes. In M. C. Wittrock (Ed.), *Handbook of research on teaching*, 3rd ed. (pp. 255–96). New York: Macmillan.

Clark, C. M. & Yinger, R. J. (1987). Teacher planning. In D. C. Berliner and B. V. Rosenshine (Eds.), *Talks to teachers: A festschrift for N. L. Gage* (pp. 342–65). New York: Random House.

Connell, R. W., Ashenden, D. J., Kessler, S., & Dowsett, G. W. (1982). *Making the difference: Schools, families and social division*. London: George Allen & Unwin.

Corcoran, E. (1981). Position shock: The beginning teacher's paradox. *The Journal of Teacher Education, 32*(3), 19–23.

Crow, N. (1987). Socialization within a teacher education program: A case study. Unpublished doctoral dissertation, University of Utah, Salt Lake City, Utah.

Darling-Hammond, L. (1985). Valuing teachers: The making of a profession. *Teachers College Record*, 87(2), 205–18.

Darling-Hammond, L. & Berry, B. (1988). *The evolution of teacher policy*. Santa Monica, California: The RAND Corporation, Center for the Study of the Teaching Profession.

Doyle, W. (1983). Academic work. *Review of Educational Research*, 53(2), 159–99.

Doyle, W. (1986). Classroom organization and management. In M. C. Wittrock (Ed.), *Handbook of research on teaching*, 3rd ed. (pp. 392–431). New York: Macmillan.

Farber, B. A. (1984). Teacher burnout: Assumptions, myths, and issues. *Teachers College Record*, 86(2), 321–38.

Freedman, S., Jackson, J., & Boles, K. (1983). The other end of the corridor: The effect of teaching on teachers. *Radical Teacher*, summer.

Fuller, F. F. & Brown, O. H. (1975). Becoming a teacher. In K. Ryan (Ed.), *Teacher education* (Seventy-fourth Yearbook of the National Society for the Study of Education) (pp. 25–52). Chicago: University of Chicago Press.

Galvez-Hjornevik, C. (1986). Mentoring among teachers: A review of the literature. *The Journal of Teacher Education*, 37(1), 6–11.

Gitlin, A. & Bullough, R. V. Jr. (1987). Teacher evaluation and empowerment: Challenging the taken-for-granted view of teaching. *Educational Policy*, 1(2), 229–47.

Goffman, E. (1959). *The presentation of self in everyday life*. Garden City, New York: Doubleday Anchor Books, Chapter 6.

Good, T. L. & Brophy, J. (1987). *Looking in classrooms*, 4th ed. New York: Harper & Row.

Goodlad, J. I. (1984). *A place called school: Prospects for the future*. New York: McGraw-Hill.

Goodman, J. (1985). Field-based experience: A study of social control and student teachers' response to institutional constraints. *Journal of Education for Teaching*, 11(1), 26–49.

Grant, L. & Rothenberg, J. (1986). The social enhancement of ability differences: Teacher-student interactions in first- and second-grade reading groups. *The Elementary School Journal*, 87(1), 29–49.

Hegler, K. & Dudley, R. (1987). Beginning teacher induction: A progress report. *The Journal of Teacher Education*, 38(1), 53–56.

The Holmes Group. (1986). *Tomorrow's teachers: A report of the Holmes Group*. East Lansing, Michigan: Michigan State University College of Education.

Kauchak, D. & Eggen, P. (in press). *Learning and teaching: Research-based methods*. Boston: Allyn & Bacon.

Kindsvatter, R., Wilen, W., & Ishler, M. (1988). Dynamics of effective teaching. White Plains, New York: Longman Inc.

Kounin, J. (1970). *Discipline and group management*. New York: Holt, Rinehart & Winston.

Lortie, D. (1975). *Schoolteacher: A sociological study*. Chicago: The University of Chicago Press.

May, W. T. (1986). Teaching students how to plan: The dominant model and alternatives. *The Journal of Teacher Education*, 37(6), 6–134.

McCutcheon, G. (1982). How do elementary school teachers plan?: The nature of planning and influences on it. In W. Doyle & T. Good (Eds.), *Focus on teaching: Readings from the elementary school journal* (pp. 260–79). Chicago: The University of Chicago Press.

The NETWORK, Inc. (1987). *A compendium of innovative teacher education projects*. Andover, Massachusetts: The NETWORK, Inc.

Oakes, J. (1985). *Keeping track: How schools structure inequality*. New Haven: Yale University Press.

Pollard, A. (1982). A model of classroom coping strategies. *British Journal of Sociology of Education*, 3(1), 19–37.

Ryan, K. (1986). The induction of new teachers. Bloomington, Indiana: Phi Delta Kappa Educational Foundation.

Schon, D. (1987). *Educating the reflective practitioner*. San Francisco: Jossey-Bass.

Shulman, J. H. & Colbert, J. A. (Eds.). (1987). *The mentor teacher casebook*. San Francisco and Eugene, Oregon: The Far West Laboratory for Educational Research and Development and the ERIC Clearinghouse on Educational Management.

Shulman, L. S. (1986). Paradigms and research programs in the study of teaching: A contemporary perspective. In M. C. Wittrock (Ed.), *Handbook of research on teaching*, 3rd ed. (pp. 3–36). New York: Macmillan.

The Task Force on Teaching as a Profession (1986). *A nation prepared: Teachers for the 21st century*. New York: The Carnegie Forum on Education and the Economy.

Veenman, S. (1984). Perceived problems of beginning teachers. *Review of Educational Research*, 54(2), 143–78.

Wise, A. E., Darling-Hammond, L., McLaughlin, M. W., & Bernstein, H. T. (1984). *Case studies for teacher evaluation: A study of effective practices*. Santa Monica, California: The RAND Corporation.

Woolever, R. M. (1985). State-mandated performance evaluation of beginning teachers: Implications for teacher educators. *The Journal of Teacher Education*, 36(2), 22–25.

Zeichner, K. M. (1986). Teacher socialization research and the practice of teaching. *Education and Society*, 3(3/2–4/1), 25–37.

Index

About the Author

Robert V. Bullough, Jr. is Associate Professor of Educational Studies, University of Utah, Salt Lake City, Utah. Since completing his Ph.D. at The Ohio State University, he has done postdoctoral study at the University of Illinois, Champaign-Urbana, and has taught and published in the areas of curriculum history, criticism and theory, and teacher education. His major areas of interest are curriculum studies and teacher education, with particular emphasis on the effects of school structure and work relations on teachers' thinking and professional development. Dr. Bullough is the author of *The Forgotten Dream of American Public Education*, and coauthor of *Human Interests in the Curriculum: Teaching and Learning in a Technological Society*. *First-Year Teacher: A Case Study* grew out of his interest in the socialization and professional development of beginning teachers, and his belief that teacher education does make a positive contribution to their development. The father of four children, Robert Bullough also enjoys gardening, house and furniture restoration, and book collecting.